The
FAR
EASTERN
MENU

▲▲▲▲▲▲▲▲▲▲▲▲▲▲▲▲▲▲▲▲▲

Cookbook

The
FAR
EASTERN
MENU

▲▲▲▲▲▲▲▲▲▲▲▲▲▲▲▲▲▲▲▲▲

Cookbook

Jacki Pan-Passmore

CASSELL

A CASSELL BOOK

First published in the UK 1993
by Cassell
Villiers House
41/47 Strand
London
WC2N 5JE

British Library Cataloguing-in-Publication Data
A catalogue record for this book is available from the British Library

ISBN 0-304-34386-2

Typeset in Cochin and Lithos
Produced by Mandarin Offset, Hong Kong

Acknowledgements

The Bay Tree Kitchen Shop

James Morland Interiors

Home Sweet Home

Art & Frame International
Double Bay, Sydney

Lamma Tai
Paddington, Sydney

Limoges Australia
Surry Hills, Sydney

Villeroy & Boch, Australia Pty Ltd
Brookvale, Sydney

CONTENTS

▲▲▲▲▲▲

Introduction 6

INTRODUCTION

▲▲▲▲▲▲

This cookbook contains a collection of delicious Asian recipes with many fresh and exciting dishes combined in twenty selected menus.

I have eaten and cooked countless Asian dishes since my first revolutionary taste of satay and Singapore chili crab in a barn-like restaurant at Changhi Beach in Singapore - en route to a new life in Hong Kong. Asian food became, within weeks of this auspicious meal, more than just a passion, but also my entry into a career from which my interest has not waned, even momentarily, in over twenty years.

I entertain frequently, from simple meals with close friends or family, to sit-down meals for thirty or more. My menus are planned around a busy working schedule. Asian food, I am delighted to say, is ideal for those of us who prefer to entertain at home.

There can be a profusion of tastes in an Asian menu. Cleverly combined, the meal will be memorable. Asians of all nationalities, and Chinese in particular, enjoy their food enormously. While eating one meal, they will plan the next. Any occasion is an excuse for a meal, or a banquet, and the menu, however small or grand, is planned with almost fanatical enthusiasm and precision.

A recent trip to the Mediterranean vividly brought back memories of an evening at an open-air restaurant in Macao, a speck of Portugal tacked onto the China coast in a time warp of vino verdi (spritzy white wine) and bacalhau (salt cod), of cobbled streets and grape vines. I have not forgotten the little bundle of Thai birdseye chilies I dared not eat, but secreted in my napkin during a particularly fiery meal of gai pad bai kaprow (finely diced chicken sauteed with basil leaves and incendiary chilies) in Bangkok. Or the lobster that fought with the chef on its way to the wok, and ended up on my plate as raw, semi-opaque slivers in a dressing that epitomises Thai tastes – lime juice, coriander and fish sauce.

When I close my eyes, my nostrils still twitch to the allure of an elusive, nutty-smoky aroma that is coconut leaves burning and coconut oil frying. It reaches out to you from a street corner in Malaysia, surprises you on a country road in Java, tempts you from a clutch of thatch huts in Ubud. It led me to a restaurant near Sanur Beach in Bali, to my first rijstaffel and the realization that I was embarked upon the most wonderful journey of discovery.

I have adopted the intense concentration the Chinese afford their food at a banquet; the reverent spooning of the shark's fin soup; the meticulous selection of a sliver of golden skin from the roast suckling pig; the slurpy appreciation of the soup or noodles;

chopsticks 'falling like rain' amidst flying elbows, raised glasses and non-stop chatter.

This book has evolved from the various dinner parties that I have created over the years. Friends loved the first mini-rijstaffel I cooked after one of my frequent sojourns to Bali, so it became a regular event. I found stir-fries great when time and the contents of the refrigerator were limited. My Indian cooking teacher and stand-in Asian mother, Daljit Singh, showed me short cuts that could put a curry on the table in minutes for unexpected guests. I returned home to Hong Kong, then to London and later to Australia, with herbs and spices from Vietnam, Laos, the Philippines and Japan so I could reproduce the dishes I had discovered on my travels. Many regularly appear on our table, and are always appreciated. I am also delighted with the range of fresh, packaged and dried ingredients now available at most good Asian food stockists.

When you are entertaining people at home, it is especially important to feel confident about the choices you are about to offer. I have always believed that the cook should enjoy the occasion as much as his or her guests, so don't try to do more than is comfortable. I have planned a variety of menus and cuisine styles which can be suited to many different occasions. But in Asian cooking, no rule is etched in stone. Feel free to mix and match elements from one menu with another.

Each menu starts with an introduction describing the recipes, the blending of their particular tastes and textures and how to serve them. Some hints on advance planning and precooking are included as well as suggestions for beverages that would suit the food and the occasion.

The first five menus are designed for easy entertaining and provide simple, attractive meals that can be prepared with minimum fuss for maximum effect. The next three menus are designed especially for tabletop cooking, where your guests can join in and become cooks if they wish. They are particularly suited to hosts who like to prepare absolutely everything in advance.

A Thai Lunch, *Dinner in Java* and *A Night in Singapore* have been created to help you make the most of lunching and dining with friends. They are trouble-free to prepare and have that touch of the East that will intrigue and impress your guests.

The following three menus have been created with a special emphasis on lightness and a subtle balance of tastes. It is fitting that they include one meal that is completely vegetarian.

In a later segment, four menus – *Indonesian Rijstaffel,*
A Night in Bangkok, The Spices of Sichuan and *Delicacies from Japan* –

concentrate on entertaining, dipping into the cuisines of four Asian countries to find combinations of old and original dishes, to form feasts for the table. You can serve these meals casually, or make them unashamedly grandiose and exotic.

Finally, two menus are included especially for party planners. Cooking for a group of friends is easy if you make the right choices from the start.

Asian food has many advantages. It adds the element of surprise, since often you are introducing guests to completely new dishes and there are fail-safe dishes that can be made in advance – a must when you invite lots of people. The size and flavor of many Asian dishes makes them ideal for finger food.

You may prefer to serve some of these menus outdoors. Eating alfresco is popular in southeast Asia – on fold-out stools around a satay vendor's stand, in bamboo chairs under a shady tree, at a bench or a table on the sand with warm tropical waters lapping at the toes, or at a kitchen table brought outdoors to catch the breezes on a humid day.

Outdoor entertaining is informal and a little contrived scene-setting with cushions, baskets and caneware, greenery, tropical flowers and ethnic tableware can transform a casual meal into a memorable event.

Each of these menus would be equally special served as an elegant luncheon or dinner in a formal setting. A good way to give interest and atmosphere to the table is with a striking table arrangement of exotic fruit or vegetables, whole spices such as nutmegs, bay leaves, cinnamon sticks and peppercorns on their branches. In addition to bright flowers, you can trail ivy or jasmine across the table, or float candles in flat glass dishes with camellias. Use woven cane or  straw mats, with Oriental figurines, cruets or candle holders to create the right mood.

In many Asian countries a platter of fresh fruit is all that is required at the end of a meal. I have given a suggestion or recipe with each menu but, if time is short, simply bring out whole or sliced fresh fruit.

Enjoy the tastes and ideas served up in this book and add your own imagination to fashion meals that you will want to create again and again.

STIR-FRY SIMPLICITY

Serves 4

Shredded Pork and Beansprouts

Stir-fried Chicken with Celery, Peppers and Peanuts

Steamed Rice

Chilled Liqueur Oranges

Stir-fry cooking has several advantages. The ingredients can be prepared in advance to make cooking time no more than a few minutes, dishes are economical, and the quick cooking ensures minimum loss of nutrients. Recipes for stir-fries can often be adapted to suit whatever the refrigerator yields, a bonus when time and budget are short.

A simple Chinese family meal is usually made up of two or three dishes containing meat or seafood and vegetables. The object is to create contrast by combining a mild dish with a more highly seasoned one. In this menu the delicacy and lightness of the pork and beansprouts, a typical Cantonese dish, are complemented by the brighter tones and piquant taste of the chicken dish which is enlivened with aromatic brown peppercorns from Sichuan and a hot chili sauce.

Steamed white rice usually accompanies stir-fried dishes, but you may choose to add interest to the rice by stirring in cooked green peas, baby shrimp and chopped scallions (spring onions).

This easy menu for four can be on the table from start to finish in twenty minutes. Put the rice on to cook while you assemble and prepare the ingredients. Prepare and chill the oranges, then cook the two dishes one after the other in a wok or large sauté pan, and take them directly to the table.

I always enjoy tea with Chinese meals. The

13

lighter green teas, plain or scented with jasmine blossoms, are refreshing, and they cleanse the palate to enable you to enjoy the characteristics of each dish. Chinese black teas such as bo lay, also known as pu erh, and the more subtle sow mai, aid the digestive process.

Shredded Pork and Beansprouts

▲▲▲▲▲▲

½ lb (250 g) lean pork
1 tablespoon cornstarch (cornflour)
1 tablespoon light soy sauce
⅓ teaspoon white pepper
3 thin slices fresh ginger
2 scallions (spring onions)
6 oz (180 g) fresh beansprouts
3 tablespoons vegetable oil
1 teaspoon sesame oil
½ cup (3 fl oz / 90 ml) chicken stock
1½ teaspoons cornstarch (cornflour)

Slice the pork, stack slices together and cut into narrow shreds, place in a dish with cornstarch, soy and pepper, mix well and marinate for 30 minutes.

Cut ginger into fine shreds. Trim scallions, cut into 1½ inch (4 cm) pieces and shred lengthwise. Break roots and seed pods from beansprouts and rinse. Drain well.

In a wok or sauté pan heat the oils together until very hot. Add pork and stir-fry quickly until it changes appearance. Add the ginger, scallions and beansprouts and stir-fry for 2 minutes on high heat. Add chicken stock and cornstarch, stir on high heat until sauce coats the ingredients.

Steamed Rice

▲▲▲▲▲▲

In a heavy-based pan with a tight-fitting lid, combine 3 parts unwashed white rice to 4 parts cold water. Cover and bring rapidly to the boil, reduce heat to the absolute minimum setting and allow the pan to sit undisturbed for at least 15 minutes. Allow ½ cup uncooked rice per serve.

SHREDDED PORK AND BEANSPROUTS

STIR-FRIED CHICKEN WITH CELERY, PEPPERS AND PEANUTS

Stir-fried Chicken with Celery, Peppers and Peanuts

▲▲▲▲▲▲

14 oz (420 g) chicken breasts
1 tablespoon cornstarch (cornflour)
salt and white pepper
2 celery stalks
½ red pepper (capsicum)
½ green or yellow pepper (capsicum)
1-2 cloves garlic
1 small onion
3 tablespoons vegetable oil
½ teaspoon crushed Sichuan brown peppercorns
3 tablespoons skinned raw peanuts
1 teaspoon hot chili sauce
½ cup (4 fl oz / 125 ml) chicken stock

Cut the chicken into ¾ inch (2 cm) cubes and mix with cornstarch and seasonings. Set aside for 10 minutes.

Slice the celery diagonally. Trim stem, seeds and inner ribs from peppers and cut into squares. Peel and sliver the garlic. Peel onion, trim root and top and cut vertically into curved slices.

Heat oil in a wok or large sauté pan over high heat. Add brown peppercorns and peanuts and cook until peanuts are golden, remove.

Add the chicken and stir-fry until it changes appearance, move to the side of the pan. Add onion and celery and stir-fry until it begins to soften. Add garlic and peppers, cook briefly, then mix the contents of the pan together and continue to stir-fry for 2 minutes.

Add chili sauce and chicken stock and cook to boiling point. Return the peppercorns and peanuts and serve.

Chilled Liqueur Oranges

▲▲▲▲▲▲

4 large oranges
1½ tablespoons orange liqueur or Cognac
whipped cream (optional)

Peel the oranges removing as much of the white pith and internal membrane as possible. Cut into thin slices. Arrange on dessert plates, overlapping the slices. Sprinkle with the liqueur and chill. Serve with whipped cream.

CHILLED LIQUEUR ORANGES

CHINESE IN A MOMENT

Serves 4

Chicken Creamed Corn Soup

Hot Chili Shrimp

Stir-fried Vegetables

Vanilla Ice Cream with Ginger Syrup

This menu begins with a mild, creamy classic soup. To stimulate the palate, it is followed with more assertive tastes and balanced by crunchy textures.

Soups are not usually served at the beginning of a Chinese meal, with the exception of shark, fin or other feature soups containing expensive ingredients which the host may choose to serve first for impact. However, you may prefer to serve it before the main dishes. Have soy sauce on the table in a small shaker bottle; a few drops brings out the full character.

I have chosen a main course of crisp fresh shrimp with pungent garlic and chili, and added the crunch of a profusion of vegetables to complete the range of textures. No additional challenges to the palate are required, so the accompaniment should be plain white rice. Sliced white fish – flour-coated and crisped in oil – could replace the shrimp for a more economical dish. This trio will cook in minutes, so have the rice already on to steam before you begin.

This easy menu deserves a quick and tasty dessert. Finely chop several tablespoons of ginger in syrup and serve over vanilla ice cream or ice cream and warmed crepes.

'Rice pattern' china, with its indigo border and translucent imprint of rice grains on the body of the dishes, is a popular table setting which I often use. For this meal you will need both soup

17

and rice bowls, porcelain spoons and chopsticks.

I would offer tea during a simple family meal, or a light dry white wine.

CHICKEN CREAMED CORN SOUP

Chicken Creamed Corn Soup

▲▲▲▲▲▲

½ lb (250 g) skinless chicken breast
1 tablespoon Chinese shaohsing wine
or dry sherry
12 oz (350 g) can corn kernels
5 cups (40 fl oz / 1250 ml) chicken stock
salt and white pepper
2 tablespoons cornstarch (cornflour)
2 large eggs
1 tablespoon finely minced ham
thinly sliced shallots

Coarsely mince (grind) the chicken and season with the wine or sherry, set aside.

Drain the corn and place in a food processor or blender with 1 cup of the stock. Process briefly to break up the grains without reducing them to a puree. Transfer to a saucepan and add the remaining stock.

Bring to the boil and simmer briefly, add salt and pepper to taste. Stir the chicken into the stock and cook on moderate heat for 5 minutes. Combine cornstarch with cold water to make a thin paste, pour into the soup and stir until it has thickened and turned slightly translucent.

In a small bowl whisk the eggs until well blended. Pour into the soup in a thin stream, it will cook into thin threads in the hot stock. Serve garnished with the minced ham and shallots.

Hot Chili Shrimp

▲▲▲▲▲▲

12 medium-large fresh shrimp in their shells
1 fresh red chili pepper
2 cloves garlic
2 scallions (spring onions)
3 tablespoons vegetable oil
salt and pepper

Shell the shrimp leaving their tails on. Open down the middle-backs, cutting deeply so the shrimp will curl when cooked. Remove dark vein. Rinse and dry shrimp.

Slit open and deseed the chili and chop coarsely. Peel garlic and cut into slivers, trim scallions and cut into 1½ inch (4 cm) lengths.

Heat oil in a wok or pan and stir-fry garlic, chili and scallions briefly. Push to one side. Add the shrimp and stir-fry until pink and barely cooked through. Add salt and pepper, mix with the other ingredients and serve at once.

HOT CHILI SHRIMP

Stir-fried Vegetables

▲▲▲▲▲▲

2-3 tablespoons vegetable oil
1 medium onion, cut into wedges
1 medium carrot, thinly sliced
2 celery sticks, thinly sliced on the diagonal
1 red pepper (capsicum), cut into squares
12 broccoli or cauliflower flowerets
3 oz (90 g) canned baby corn, drained
2 oz (60 g) sliced bamboo shoots, drained
2 oz (60 g) canned straw mushrooms, halved
1½ tablespoons light soy sauce
¾ cup (6 fl oz / 180 ml) chicken stock
2 teaspoons cornstarch (cornflour)
salt and pepper

Place a wok on a tabletop cooker and add the oil. Heat well, then stir-fry the onion, carrot and celery for 2 minutes. Add red pepper and broccoli or cauliflower, and stir-fry briefly, then add 2 tablespoons of cold water, cover the pan and cook for 3 minutes.

Add the canned vegetables and sauce and the stock mixed with cornstarch and cook on high heat, stirring until the sauce thickens. Season to taste and serve.

STIR-FRIED VEGETABLES

QUICK-COOK THAI

Serves 4

*Chicken and Ginger Soup with
Coconut Milk*

*Thai Noodles with Seafood
and Roast Pork*

*Sliced Beef, Mushrooms and Vegetables
in Oyster Sauce*

Tropical Fruit Salad

Authentic Thai character can be achieved
in minutes with these simple recipes which
are all relatively mild in taste. Lime and lemon,
and plenty of fresh-tasting ginger – the Thais
use a mild local ginger in abundance in many of
their dishes – balance the creaminess of the
coconut soup.

Not all Thai dishes are hot or spicy, and many
are Chinese in origin. Seafood and meats
combine in the noodle dish which is substantial
and varied enough to require a simple
accompaniment like this Chinese inspired beef
and mushroom dish. Serve a bowl of white rice
with the beef and have a shaker bottle of Thai
fish sauce and a pot of chili sauce on the table for
those who prefer their food hotter.

Chinese-style tableware, with chopsticks,
could be used for this menu, although Thais
traditionally eat from small dinner plates using a
fork and spoon. Small effort for maximum
reward, this is a menu to suit many occasions.

The refreshing tang of fresh lime juice over
ice, sweetened with sugar, is a cooling drink that
is enjoyed in many parts of southeast Asia. Make
it up in tall glasses to serve with your Thai meals,
and if you want to offer a wine consider a lightly
chilled beaujolais or rosé.

Chicken and Ginger Soup with Coconut Milk

▲▲▲▲▲▲

2 chicken thighs and drumsticks (maryland)
1 lemon grass stalk, trimmed, or 2 tablespoons dried lemon grass
3 dried Kaffir lime leaves, soaked
1 inch (2.5 cm) piece fresh ginger, thickly sliced
1 fresh green chili, seeded
2 scallions (spring onions)
14 fl oz (440 ml) can thick coconut milk (cream)
Thai fish sauce and lime juice to taste
salt and white pepper
12 sprigs of fresh coriander

Place the chicken in a saucepan with 4 cups water and bring almost to the boil. Add lemon grass, lime leaves and ginger. Simmer (without allowing to boil) for 20 minutes, skimming occasionally.

Remove chicken skin, debone and cut the meat into small cubes. Strain the broth into a clean saucepan, adding the ginger slices.

Roughly chop the chili and cut scallions into 1 inch (2.5 cm) lengths, add to the soup with cubed chicken and coconut milk. Bring just to the boil and simmer for 6-7 minutes.

Add fish sauce, lime juice and seasonings to taste. Stir in coriander and serve at once.

CHICKEN AND GINGER SOUP WITH COCONUT MILK

THAI NOODLES WITH SEAFOOD AND ROAST PORK

Thai Noodles with Seafood and Roast Pork

▲▲▲▲▲▲

8 oz (250 g) rice stick noodles

5 oz (150 g) chicken breast

12 fresh sea scallops

2 medium squid, cleaned and cut into rings

1 medium onion, cut into narrow wedges

2 scallions (spring onions), sliced

1 small red pepper (capsicum), sliced

4 tablespoons vegetable oil

2 cloves garlic, finely chopped

4 oz (120 g) fresh beansprouts

6 oz (180 g) Chinese style roast pork, shredded

2 tablespoons Thai fish sauce

½ teaspoon white pepper

1 fresh red chili pepper, seeded and shredded

salt to taste

Soak the rice sticks in hot water to soften. Cut the chicken into small cubes. Prepare the seafood and vegetables.

Heat half the oil in a wok or large sauté pan. Stir-fry the chicken, onions and red pepper for 2-3 minutes. Add seafood and stir-fry until lightly cooked. Remove and keep warm.

Drain the noodles thoroughly. Add remaining oil to the pan and heat. Add the noodles, beansprouts and garlic and stir-fry for 2 minutes, then return the cooked ingredients and add the roast pork, fish sauce and seasonings, stir in chili. Mix well and stir-fry for 1-2 minutes.

SLICED BEEF, MUSHROOMS AND VEGETABLES IN OYSTER SAUCE

Sliced Beef, Mushrooms and Vegetables in Oyster Sauce

▲▲▲▲▲▲

1 lb (500 g) rump steak
1½ tablespoons cornstarch (cornflour)
2 tablespoons Thai fish sauce
3 teaspoons sugar
¾ lb (375 g) Chinese green vegetables
3 tablespoons vegetable oil
4 scallions (spring onions), cut into
1 inch (2.5 cm) lengths
4 oz (125 g) can baby champignons, drained
¾ cup (6 fl oz / 185 ml) beef stock
white pepper to taste
2 tablespoons oyster sauce

Very thinly slice the beef (best done if partially frozen) and cut into strips. Place in a dish and sprinkle on 1 tablespoon cornstarch, the fish sauce and sugar. Mix well and marinate for 10 minutes.

Cut the vegetables into 3 inch (8 cm) pieces and blanch in boiling water for 3 minutes. Drain.

Heat the oil in a wok or large sauté pan and stir-fry the beef until it changes appearance. Add the onion and champignons and the beef stock mixed with remaining cornstarch. Stir over high heat until the sauce thickens. Add the vegetables and heat through in the sauce. Stir in white pepper, transfer to a serving dish and pour the oyster sauce evenly over the dish.

Tropical Fruit Salad

▲▲▲▲▲▲

½ honeydew melon
½ cantaloupe (rockmelon)
¼ small watermelon
1 firm pear
1 small can sliced mango in syrup
1 can passionfruit pulp, or the pulp and juice
of 3 passionfruit
1 carambola or a small bunch of fresh lychees
2 soft bananas
¾ cup thickened (heavy) cream
juice of 1 small lime

Peel the melons and use a melon scoop to cut into balls. Core and thinly slice the pear.

Combine the prepared fruit in a glass bowl and add the mango and its liquid, and the passionfruit. Stir lightly. Decorate the dish with sliced carambola or the bunch of fresh lychees.

Mash the bananas to a smooth puree. Whip the cream until thick, fold in the banana and lime juice. Serve separately.

TROPICAL FRUIT SALAD

TWENTY MINUTE THAI CURRY

Serves 4

*Thai-style Carpaccio of Beef
with Salad Greens*

Thai Green Curry Paste

Green Shrimp Curry

Egg Crepe

*Iced Coconut Milk
with Water Chestnuts*

The unforgettable taste of Thai food can be achieved without lengthy preparation if you choose a menu which uses classic seasonings. The Thai-style Carpaccio of raw beef, shaved paper thin, dressed with fresh lime juice, fish sauce, pepper and coriander, is edged by a border of fresh oriental herbs and salad greens.

The main course is a quick-to-prepare curry of plump shrimp bathed in a vibrant coconut curry sauce of decisive heat. It features lime and herbs, but in this dish they serve to lend characteristic Thai aromas rather than dominant taste. The dish can be made with a bottled curry paste for ease and speed, but if you plan ahead, you can make up the wonderfully rich Thai Green Curry Paste, and keep what's left in the refrigerator for another occasion.

Serve the curry with white rice cooked by the absorption method, but using the thin long grain white rice the Thais call Jasmine. In Thailand, the rice is often garnished with fine shreds of egg crepe, a few slivers of hot chili and a sprinkle of crushed roasted peanuts. Pile it in a cone shape, as they do, and drape the garnish over the top.

Palates seared by chilies need creamy desserts or drinks to cool and soothe them, therefore a

27

natural conclusion to this casual meal is to serve tall glasses of coconut milk with water chestnuts over crushed ice.

Serve one of the new styles of white wine designed to accompany Asian dishes – basically dry but with undertones of honey and spice.

Thai-style Carpaccio of Beef with Salad Greens

▲▲▲▲▲▲

10½ oz (300 g) beef fillet (tenderloin) in a single piece
2 tablespoons Thai fish sauce (nam pla)
3 tablespoons fresh lime juice
1 tablespoon brown or palm sugar
1½ tablespoons corn oil
½ teaspoon freshly milled black pepper
1 tablespoon chopped fresh coriander
2 tablespoons thinly sliced shallot tops
1 tablespoon crushed roasted peanuts
assorted salad greens
fresh mint leaves
fresh basil leaves
fresh coriander leaves

Using a thin bladed sharp knife or Chinese cleaver cut the meat across the grain into paper-thin slices (partially freezing will make this easier). Arrange them, overlapped, on large dinner plates.

Combine the fish sauce, lime juice, palm sugar and oil, whisking until well blended. Sprinkle half over the beef and add pepper, chopped coriander, shallots and peanuts.

Wash and dry the salad greens and herbs, arrange in a ring around the beef on each plate and drizzle on remaining dressing.

Steamed white rice is a traditional accompaniment to this kind of meal. Make it by your preferred method.

Thai Green Curry Paste

▲▲▲▲▲▲

1 teaspoon black peppercorns
1½ teaspoons coriander seeds
3 cloves garlic
2 lemon grass stems (white part only)
1 cup (1 oz / 30 g) loosely packed fresh coriander
½ cup (45 g) chopped scallions (spring onions)
1 inch (2.5 cm) piece fresh ginger, peeled
1 teaspoon ground galangal
3-6 fresh green chilies, seeded
2 teaspoons sugar

Toast the peppercorns and coriander seeds in a dry pan until they are very aromatic, then grind finely. Pulverize the remaining ingredients in a heavy-duty food processor, adding the spices.

To make the curry paste in advance, grind as above, then fry for 4-5 minutes in 3 tablespoons oil. It may be refrigerated for up to 3 weeks.

THAI-STYLE CARPACCIO OF BEEF WITH SALAD GREENS

GREEN SHRIMP CURRY

Green Shrimp Curry

▲▲▲▲▲▲

1¼ lb (650 g) fresh large shrimp in their shells
1 recipe green Thai curry paste or ½–1 ½
tablespoons bottled Thai curry paste
3 tablespoons vegetable oil
3 dried Kaffir lime leaves, soaked in 1 cup
(8 fl oz / 250 ml) boiling water
14 fl oz (440 ml) can thick coconut
milk (cream)
1 cup (1 oz / 30 g) loosely packed fresh
basil leaves
salt and white pepper
Thai fish sauce and lime juice to taste

Shell the shrimp, leaving their tails on (Thais would also leave on the heads to give extra richness to the dish). Set aside. Sauté the curry paste in the same oil for 4-5 minutes until it is very aromatic.

Add the lime leaves in their soaking water and the coconut milk and simmer for 10 minutes, stirring occasionally. Add the shrimp and cook gently until tender – about 10 minutes. Add the basil and seasonings to taste.

Egg Crepe

▲▲▲▲▲▲

Rub the inner surface of a wok or non-stick pan with a lightly oiled cloth or piece of kitchen towel. Heat the pan well. Beat 1-2 eggs and pour into the hot pan, swirling it around so it forms a thin crepe. Cook briefly, then flip and lightly cook the other side. Remove and leave to cool before rolling up to shred finely. Scatter over cooked rice vermicelli.

ICED COCONUT MILK WITH WATER CHESTNUTS

Iced Coconut Milk with Water Chestnuts

▲▲▲▲▲▲

14 fl oz (440 ml) can thick coconut milk (cream)
small pinch of salt
2 tablespoons sugar syrup
crushed ice
1 small can sliced water chestnuts

In a jug or bowl combine the coconut cream, salt and sugar syrup. Half fill tall glasses with crushed ice, and divide the water chestnuts between them.

Pour on the coconut milk and serve.

AN EASY INDIAN MEAL

Serves 4-6

Tangy Fruit and Vegetable Salad

Creamy Yogurt Chicken Curry

Spiced Lentils

Cheese and Spinach

Almond Saffron Rice

Chupatis

Cardamom Rice Pudding

Northern Indian dishes are for those who prefer milder curries. This is a classic menu combination, beginning with a salad which combines fruits, onion and celery with the fresh taste of mint. The tangy dressing stirs the taste buds then the creamy curry, gently spiced and delicate, softens its impact. Like many curries, this Yogurt Chicken Curry is not particularly visually inspiring, so I have teamed it with golden saffron rice with toasted nuts for eye and appetite appeal. The rice pudding with cardamom completes an interesting menu.

Prepare a tray containing small bowls of spicy pickles and chutneys, diced cucumber in natural yogurt and sliced onion marinated in salt and vinegar. Chupatis would round out the menu, but they take time to make. Unleavened pita bread, brushed with butter, sprinkled with spices and crisped in a hot oven, are an excellent stand-in.

Alcohol is rarely drunk in India, and this typical menu is not well suited to wine. Prepare instead a punch of fruit juices with a splash of liquor, or offer chilled light beer.

Tangy Fruit and Vegetable Salad

▲▲▲▲▲▲

1 large onion, sliced
2 teaspoons salt
2 tablespoons white vinegar
1½ tablespoons sugar
2 red apples, sliced
1 large pear, sliced
2 celery stalks, sliced
2 slices pineapple, cubed
1 teaspoon finely chopped fresh red chili
2 teaspoons finely chopped fresh mint

In a small bowl combine onion and salt and set aside for 10 minutes, then knead the onion slices gently with the fingers to soften, rinse quickly and drain.

Pour vinegar and sugar over the onion and set aside while the remaining salad ingredients are prepared.

Combine the salad ingredients, which should taste quite tangy. Chill slightly before serving.

TANGY FRUIT AND VEGETABLE SALAD

CREAMY YOGURT CHICKEN CURRY

Creamy Yogurt Chicken Curry

▲▲▲▲▲▲

2 lb (1 kg) chicken pieces
1 fresh green chili, seeded
1⅕ inch (3 cm) piece fresh ginger
4 cloves garlic, peeled
salt and black pepper
1 cup (8 fl oz / 250 ml) natural yogurt
2 teaspoons garam masala spice mix
1½ teaspoons ground turmeric
2-3 tablespoons vegetable oil or ghee
(clarified butter)
1 cup (8 oz / 250 g) pureed seeded tomatoes
3 tablespoons chopped fresh coriander
5 scallions (spring onions), chopped
2 tablespoons thick (heavy) cream

Cut the chicken into small serving pieces and place in a dish.

In a spice grinder or food processor grind the chili, ginger and garlic to a paste, add pepper and yogurt and mix well. Spread over the chicken and set aside for 1 hour (this can be done in advance and the chicken refrigerated for up to 2 days). Sprinkle on the spices.

Heat the oil or ghee in a saucepan, add the chicken and cook on medium heat to brown slightly. Take care the spices do not burn. Add the tomatoes, cover the pan and cook until the chicken is tender and the sauce has reduced to a thick paste.

Stir in the coriander, scallions and cream and simmer a further 3-4 minutes, stirring to prevent food from catching on the pan. Check seasonings.

Spiced Lentils

▲▲▲▲▲▲

1¼ cup (8 oz / 250 g) lentils
2 teaspoons salt
1 fresh green chili, seeded and chopped
1 teaspoon ground turmeric
3 tablespoons butter or ghee
1 medium onion, chopped finely
½ teaspoon black mustard seeds (optional)
1 teaspoon crushed garlic
1 teaspoon crushed ginger
1 large tomato, seeded and chopped finely
2 teaspoons garam masala spice mix
1 teaspoon ground coriander
2 teaspoons finely chopped fresh coriander

Rinse and thoroughly drain the lentils and place them in a saucepan with the salt, chili and turmeric. Add 4 cups water and bring to the boil. Partially cover the pan and simmer for about 20 mintues until the lentils are tender. Drain well.

In another pan heat the butter and sauté the onion to a golden brown. Add the mustard seeds, garlic and ginger and sauté briefly. Add tomato and cook on low heat to a thick puree.

Stir in the drained lentils, add spices and coriander and cook together for 2-3 minutes.

CHEESE AND SPINACH

Cheese and Spinach

▲▲▲▲▲▲

1 lb (500 g) cottage cheese
3 tablespoons ghee (clarified butter)
1 lb (500 g) fresh or frozen spinach
½ teaspoon ground nutmeg
1 clove garlic, chopped very finely
2-3 tablespoons cream
salt and pepper

Press the cottage cheese through a fine sieve onto a piece of fine clean cloth. Squeeze out as much liquid as possible from the cheese, then place it in a strainer over a bowl. Place a heavy weight on top and set aside for several hours to compress the cheese.

Form into ¾ inch (2 cm) balls. Heat ghee in a flat pan and fry the cheese balls carefully until golden on the surface. Remove.

Steam the spinach until tender. Add nutmeg, garlic, if used, and the cream, and cook gently for 1-2 minutes. Season to taste with salt and pepper. Add the cheese and gently heat through before serving.

Almond Saffron Rice

▲▲▲▲▲▲

2½ cups (18 oz / 560 g) long-grain white rice
3¼ cups (26 fl oz / 810 ml) chicken stock
1 teaspoon salt
2-3 bruised green cardamom pods
½ teaspoon powdered saffron
2 tablespoons toasted slivered almonds
1 tablespoon ghee

Combine rice, stock, salt, cardamom pods and saffron in a saucepan with a heavy base. Bring quickly to the boil, cover tightly and reduce heat to lowest setting.

Cook gently for 15 minutes, stir in almonds and ghee and cook a further 5 minutes.

Cardamom Rice Pudding

▲▲▲▲▲▲

½ cup (3 oz / 90 g) short-grain white rice
3 ¼ cups fresh full-cream milk
3 cardamom pods, crushed
2 ½ oz (75 g) white sugar
2 tablespoons chopped pistachio nuts (optional)

Rinse the rice and drain, cover with fresh water and soak for 1 hour, drain again.

In a medium saucepan bring the milk to a slow boil, add rice and cardamoms and return to the boil. Reduce heat, cover the pan and simmer until the rice is very tender.

Stir in sugar and cook a further 5 minutes. Transfer to dessert dishes and chill. Sprinkle on chopped pistachios to serve.

ALMOND SAFFRON RICE

CHUPATIS

Chupatis

▲▲▲▲▲▲

*1½ cups (8 oz / 250 g) fine wholewheat
(wholemeal) flour
3 teaspoons ghee (clarified butter)
½ cup (4 fl oz / 125 ml) lukewarm water
extra ghee for cooking*

Sift the flour into a mixing bowl and rub in the ghee. Add enough of the water to make a very stiff dough. Remove from the bowl and knead firmly on a sparsely floured board for 7 minutes. Cover with a cloth and set aside for 10 minutes, then knead again briefly.

Form into balls about the size of a golfball and roll out very thinly.

Rub the inner surface of a cast-iron or non-stick pan with a piece of paper towel dipped into softened ghee. Cook the chupatis one at a time until flecks of brown appear on the underside, turn and cook the other side. When done, they should appear slightly bubbly on the surface. Cover with a cloth to keep warm while the remainder are cooked.

SINGAPORE STEAMBOAT

Serves 8

Shrimp or Fish Balls

Singapore Steamboat Meat and Vegetable Platters

Soy Chili Sauce

Coconut Mango Jelly

I enjoy the immediacy and fun of tabletop cooking. The copper, moat-like steamboat, which sits on a heatproof mat in the middle of the table, is constructed around a central chimney with charcoal below.

You can improvize with a saucepan or heatproof casserole over a portable heat source. The pot is filled with water, and as each guest cooks his or her own portions, the broth becomes richer. When the last bite leaves the pot, the broth is served with noodles as a soup.

Equip your guests with a pair of bamboo chopsticks and one of the tiny woven wire baskets made for the steamboat. Each guest selects an ingredient and suspends it in the hot broth. They should each have a bowl in which to beat a raw egg (if they want to be authentic) for dipping. For variety, also offer hot chili and dark soy sauce, and make up a dip that is particularly popular in Singapore – soy sauce spiked with sliced green chili.

The steamboat itself makes a long, leisurely meal, so you will not need to prepare an appetizer. In Singapore, they would be happy to finish with a platter of orange wedges or chilled grapes, but I have provided a simple soothing dessert.

Offer well-chilled beer with carbonated drinks for spritzing, or a crisp dry white wine.

SHRIMP OR FISH BALLS

Shrimp or Fish Balls

▲▲▲▲▲▲

14 oz (440 g) fresh shelled shrimp or boneless,
skinless white fish
2 oz (60 g) pork fat, diced
2 teaspoons grated fresh ginger
1 tablespoon very finely chopped scallions
(spring onions)
2 egg whites
½ teaspoon sugar
½ teaspoon salt
1 tablespoon cornstarch (cornflour)

Place the ingredients in a food processor and
add 3 tablespoons water. Process to a
smooth, sticky consistency.

Bring a large pot of lightly salted water to the
boil, then reduce to a simmer. To form the balls,
take a handful of the mixture and clench the hand
gently so that a ball-shaped portion of the mixture is squeezed out above the thumb. Scoop off
with a spoon and drop into the simmering water
to cook just until they come to the surface.

Transfer cooked seafood balls to cold water,
then drain before serving with the steamboat.

Singapore Steamboat Meat and Vegetable Platters

▲▲▲▲▲▲

½ lb (250 g) beef fillet (tenderloin) in one piece
½ lb (250 g) lean pork in one piece
½ lb (250 g) boneless, skinless chicken breasts
18 medium shrimp, peeled with tails intact
1 lb (500 g) Chinese (napa) cabbage
1 lb (500 g) fresh spinach
4 squares fresh soft beancurd
4 oz (120 g) bean-thread vermicelli, soaked
4 oz (120 g) fresh beansprouts
12 dried black mushrooms, soaked
8 scallions (spring onions), trimmed
8 slices fresh ginger

Accompaniments:
6 large eggs
sesame oil
soy sauce
chili sauce
sesame sauce (thinned with water)

Trim the meat of excess fat and any surface
membranes. It will be much easier to cut into
the required paper-thin slices if the meat is frozen
until it feels firm. Using a sharp cleaver or heavy
knife, slice the meat across the grain into paper-
thin slices. Arrange them, overlapped, on two or
three platters keeping the different meats in their
individual groups.

Arrange the seafood balls and shrimp on
separate plates.

Roughly chop or slice the cabbage and
spinach. Drain mushrooms and remove stems.
Thickly slice the beancurd, and drain the
vermicelli. Arrange these ingredients and the
beansprouts on another two or three platters.

Bring a large pan of water to the boil. Place the
steamboat in the middle of the table and fill it

with glowing charcoal, or ignite an alternate heat source. Fill the steamboat with the hot water and add the scallions and ginger. Prepare the dipping sauce and accompaniments.

Cook the food briefly in the simmering broth and retrieve with chopsticks or the wire baskets. Dip before eating.

Soy Chili Sauce

▲▲▲▲▲▲

3 fresh green chilies
⅖ cup (5 fl oz / 160 ml) light soy sauce
2½ teaspoons sugar
1 tablespoon peanut oil

Slice the chilies very thinly, place in a colander and shake to remove as many of the seeds as possible. Combine with the remaining ingredients and leave for 20 minutes.

Coconut Mango Jelly

▲▲▲▲▲▲

13½ oz (345 g) can sliced mango
1 tablespoon gelatine
½ cup (4 fl oz / 125 ml) boiling water
14 fl oz (440 ml) can thick coconut milk (cream)
fresh fruit to decorate

Puree mango with its liquid. In a mixing bowl dissolve the gelatine in boiling water. Add the coconut milk and pureed mango and mix well.

Pour into dessert dishes, or into wet jelly tins and chill until firm. Serve the dishes on a plate, with sliced fresh fruit, or turn out tins and surround with the fruit. Serve chilled.

COCONUT MANGO JELLY

KOREAN BARBECUE

Serves 6-8

Green Onion, Chili and Beef Shred Soup

Vegetable Mung Bean Fritters

Korean Beef Rib Barbecue

Marinated Spinach

Fruit in Plum Wine

At a Korean barbecue, guests sizzle fragments of marinated meat or chunks of beef rib on a conical iron pan fitted snugly over a portable gas burner. The meats have been marinated in soy, wine and sesame oil, so they char appealingly on the hot surface.

I like to serve a dish that can be nibbled on while the barbecue is being prepared, so have chosen fritters of mung bean, vegetables and salty, chili-hot Korean *kim chi*, the fermented cabbage and chili pickle, for starters. They also accustom the palate to the garlic and sesame tastes that will follow. The ribs are quite robust, so serve plenty of white rice with them.

There are many different side dishes that can accompany the barbecue. I have chosen the Marinated Spinach to counteract the richness of the ribs. Other Korean delicacies could include tiny dried whitebait (available from most Asian food stockists) crisp-fried in vegetable and sesame oil; shredded nori seaweed crisped over a flame; deep-fried pinenuts; beansprouts sautéed in sesame oil, or sliced cucumber and radish pickled in vinegar with salt and sugar.

This tasty menu requires advance preparation of the marinated ribs, and the mung beans for the fritters. Serve with warmed sake, very dry sherry or martinis.

43

Green Onion, Chili and Beef Shred Soup

▲▲▲▲▲▲

1½ lb (750 g) braising steak
10 cups (80 fl oz / 2½ l) water
1 dried red chili, seeded
1¼ inch (3 cm) piece fresh ginger
4 cloves garlic, chopped
8 large scallions (spring onions)
1 tablespoon white sesame seeds
1-2 teaspoons chili powder
1 teaspoon sugar
⅓ teaspoon cracked black pepper
1 tablespoon dark soy sauce

Cut the beef into large cubes and place in a heavy stewpan with water and the dried chili and ginger. Bring to the boil, skim, then reduce heat and simmer gently for 1¾ hours until the meat is very tender and the stock has reduced by half.

Remove and drain the beef. Strain the broth into a clean pan. Trim the meat and cut or tear into narrow strips, return to the boil.

Trim the scallions, cut into 1½ inch (4 cm) pieces and shred lengthwise. Add to the soup.

Separately, toast the sesame seeds in a pan without oil until they begin to pop and are golden. Grind in a spice grinder or mortar with the chili powder, sugar and pepper.

Stir into the soup, adding soy sauce and sugar to taste. Serve.

GREEN ONION, CHILI AND BEEF SHRED SOUP

VEGETABLE MUNG BEAN FRITTERS

Vegetable Mung Bean Fritters

▲▲▲▲▲▲

*1 cup (10 oz / 310 g) dried mung beans,
soaked overnight
6 oz (180 g) kim chi (Korean pickled cabbage)
4 oz (120 g) fresh beansprouts
1 medium onion, sliced finely
6 oz (120 g) shredded eggplant or zucchini
(courgette)
2-3 cloves garlic, chopped finely
3 large eggs
½ cup self-raising flour
2 tablespoons dark soy sauce
2 teaspoons sesame oil
white pepper
vegetable oil for frying*

Drain the soaked beans, pour into a saucepan and add unsalted water to generously cover, bring to the boil and simmer until the beans are tender. Drain, return to the pan and stir over a moderate to low heat until the beans break up into a puree and are reasonably dry. Remove from the heat.

Very finely shred the kim chi, add with the remaining ingredients, except frying oil, to the bean puree and mix well.

Heat a large sauté pan and add a film of oil. Place tablespoons of the mixture in the pan and cook on moderate heat until golden brown, turn and cook other side then remove from the pan. Keep warm while the remaining mixture is cooked.

Serve warm with a dip of light soy sauce, chopped chili and fresh coriander.

KOREAN BEEF RIB BARBECUE

Korean Beef Rib Barbecue

▲▲▲▲▲▲

6 lb (3 kg) beef short ribs
1 cup (8 fl oz / 250 ml) light soy sauce
1 cup (8 fl oz / 250 ml) water
8 scallions (spring onions), chopped finely
8 cloves garlic, chopped finely
1½ inches (4 cm) fresh ginger, chopped finely
2 tablespoons sugar
1 teaspoon cracked black pepper
⅓ cup (2¾ fl oz / 85 ml) sesame oil

The ribs must be marinated overnight for maximum taste. Buy ribs which have been cut into 2 inch (5 cm) pieces, or ask your butcher to do it for you.

Use a small sharp knife to deeply score the meat between the ribs.

Place in a large shallow dish and pour on the soy sauce and water.

Prepare the scallions, ginger and garlic and scatter evenly over the meat, adding the sugar, pepper and 1 tablespoon of sesame oil. Cover with plastic wrap and refrigerate overnight.

Heat a domed Korean broiler (grill) or improvised tabletop griddle, and oil sparingly. Drain the ribs, reserving the marinade. Cook the ribs, turning frequently, until the surface is well browned and the meat is tender. During cooking, brush on the reserved marinade from time to time.

As the ribs are to be eaten from the hand, present each diner with a fingerbowl containing warm Chinese tea or warm water and lemon slices, and of course, ample napkins.

Marinated Spinach

▲▲▲▲▲▲

½ lb (250 g) fresh spinach
2 tablespoons sesame oil
2 tablespoons white sesame seeds
2 cloves garlic, crushed
1 teaspoon finely grated fresh ginger
1-2 teaspoons finely chopped fresh red chili
2 tablespoons white vinegar
3 tablespoons light soy sauce
1½-2 tablespoons sugar
salt and black pepper

Thoroughly rinse the spinach and trim stems. Tear or cut larger leaves into strips. Shake in a cloth to remove excess water. Place in a stainless steel or glass bowl and pour on the sesame oil, mix lightly, cover and set aside.

In a dry pan gently cook the sesame seeds without oil until they begin to pop and are aromatic and golden. Pour into a mortar and grind to a paste with the garlic, ginger and chili.

Combine these with vinegar, soy sauce and sugar and pour over the salad, add salt and pepper to taste and stir well. Cover and marinate for 3-4 hours before serving.

MARINATED SPINACH

Fruit in Plum Wine

▲▲▲▲▲▲

2 oranges
2 firm pears or apples
1 small melon (honeydew or cantaloupe / rockmelon)
1 medium bunch green grapes
4 plums
¼ cup (2 fl oz / 60 ml) plum wine
1 tablespoon finely chopped preserved ginger in its syrup

Peel and slice the oranges, pears or apples. Peel the melon and use a scoop to form balls, or cut into cubes. Halve the grapes and deseed, if needed. Cut the plums into quarters and discard the stones.

Combine the fruit in a bowl. Sprinkle on the wine and ginger and cover with plastic wrap. Chill for 2–3 hours before serving.

TABLETOP SIZZLER

Serves 8

Thai Shrimp in Chili and Lime Soup

Minced Pork and Chinese Sausage Served in Lettuce Cups

Sesame Lamb with Rice

Stir-fried Vegetables

Liqueur Melon with Coconut Milk

This delicious menu begins with the sharp, hot, citrus tastes of a Thai shrimp soup which can be cooked in minutes on a tabletop cooker. I have followed it with the sweet crunchiness of minced pork and Chinese vegetables seasoned with bean sauces, and wrapped in lettuce parcels. Fun to make and wonderful to eat.

Sesame lamb adds another dimension with its nutty taste. Keep it mild, or add additional chili. Prepare steamed white rice and serve it in a heat-retaining flask. This lively menu requires a simple cleansing and refreshing dessert. Melon in a mint liqueur, with coconut milk, will soothe and refresh the palate.

The simplest tabletop cooker, and probably the least expensive, is a compact gas-fired cooker onto which clips a small can of compressed gas. You can use any suitable pan or casserole, or a flat griddle over it. It will heat in seconds and a single can of gas is usually enough to cook an entire meal, or more. My cooker is fitted with a frame to support a wok, which I use for stir-fry dishes. You will need to protect your tabletop. Set the cooker on a thick ceramic tile over a heat-resistant mat.

A crisp white Sauvignon Blanc or Semillon, beaujolais or a light merlot-based blend of light red wine will enhance the flavors in this meal.

49

Thai Shrimp in Chili and Lime Soup

▲▲▲▲▲▲

1½ lb (750 g) raw shrimp in their shells
6 cups (48 fl oz / 1½ l) fish stock (broth)
4 dried Kaffir lime leaves, soaked
2 lemon grass stalks, trimmed and halved
lengthwise
½ inch (1.5 cm) piece fresh ginger, sliced
2 cloves garlic, peeled and bruised
2 fresh red chili peppers, seeded and sliced
2 tablespoons Thai fish sauce
salt and black pepper
2 small limes, quartered
2 scallions (spring onions), chopped
1 tablespoon chopped fresh coriander

Shell the shrimp leaving their tails intact. Place the heads and shells in a stewpan and add the fish stock, bring almost to the boil, then simmer for 10 minutes without allowing it to boil. Strain.

Return stock to the pan, add the drained lime leaves, lemon grass, ginger, garlic and chili. Bring to the boil and simmer for 10 minutes, then add the shrimp, fish sauce, salt, pepper and limes.

Cook briefly so the shrimp remain crisply textured. Add the scallions and coriander and serve.

THAI SHRIMP IN CHILI AND LIME SOUP

MINCED PORK AND CHINESE SAUSAGE SERVED IN LETTUCE CUPS

Minced Pork and Chinese Sausage Served in Lettuce Cups

▲▲▲▲▲▲

4 dried Chinese sausages (lap cheong)
1 lb (500 g) lean pork, coarsely
minced (ground)
3 dried black mushrooms, soaked
2 oz (60 g) canned bamboo shoots, drained
2 oz (60 g) canned straw mushrooms, drained
1 medium carrot, very finely diced
2 tablespoons vegetable oil
1 teaspoon sesame oil
1 clove garlic, chopped finely
½ inch (1.5 cm) piece fresh ginger, chopped finely
3 scallions (spring onions), chopped
1 tablespoon light soy sauce
2 tablespoons Chinese sweet bean paste
salt and pepper
12 medium sized lettuce leaves
hoisin sauce or Chinese barbecue sauce
for dipping

Place the sausages in a steamer and steam over simmering water for 10 minutes. Cool then dice finely.

Drain mushrooms and remove stems. Chop mushrooms and bamboo shoots finely. Have all the prepared ingredients and seasonings on the table.

Heat a tabletop or electric frying pan and add the oils. Stir-fry the pork and sausage until the pork changes appearance. Add the vegetables, garlic and ginger and stir-fry for 4-5 minutes until they are well cooked.

Add the scallions, sauces, salt and pepper and cook until the dish is very aromatic.

Serve the meat in lettuce cups, roll up, dip in the sauce and eat from the fingers.

Sesame Lamb

▲▲▲▲▲▲

1½ lb (750 g) lean lamb
3-4 cloves garlic, chopped finely
2 tablespoons yellow rice wine or sake
2½ tablespoons sesame oil
1 tablespoon dark soy sauce
1 tablespoon light soy sauce
3 teaspoons sugar
2 teaspoons cornstarch (cornflour)
1 large onion, sliced finely
2 tablespoons vegetable oil
1 tablespoon white sesame seeds, toasted
2 scallion (spring onion) tops, shredded
1 fresh red chili, seeded and shredded

Cut the lamb into thin slices, stack several slices together at a time and slice crosswise into very fine shreds. Place in a dish and add the garlic, wine, sesame oil, soy sauce, sugar and cornstarch. Mix well and marinate for at least 30 minutes before taking it to the table.

Heat a tabletop or electric frying pan and add the oil. Sauté the sliced onion until lightly browned, push to the side of the pan.

Add the meat, retaining any excess marinade, and cook on very high heat, stirring and turning continually until the meat is well cooked and very aromatic. Stir in the onions and any remaining marinade. Turn off the heat. The dish can be served directly from the pan into bowls of steamed white rice and garnished with the sesame seeds, scallions and chili.

SESAME LAMB

STIR-FRIED VEGETABLES

Stir-fried Vegetables

▲▲▲▲▲▲

2-3 tablespoons vegetable oil
1 medium onion, cut into wedges
1 medium carrot, thinly sliced
2 celery sticks, thinly sliced on the diagonal
1 red pepper (capsicum), cut into squares
12 broccoli or cauliflower flowerets
3 oz (90 g) canned baby corn, drained
2 oz (60 g) sliced bamboo shoots, drained
2 oz (60 g) canned straw mushrooms, halved
1½ tablespoons light soy sauce
¾ cup (6 fl oz / 180 ml) chicken stock
2 teaspoons cornstarch (cornflour)
salt and pepper

Place a wok on the tabletop cooker and add the oil. Heat well, then stir-fry the onion, carrot and celery for 2 minutes. Add red pepper and broccoli or cauliflower, and stir-fry briefly, then add 2 tablespoons of cold water, cover the pan and cook for 3 minutes.

Add the canned vegetables and sauce and the stock mixed with cornstarch and cook on high heat, stirring until the sauce thickens. Season.

Liqueur Melon with Coconut Milk

▲▲▲▲▲▲

1 cup (8 fl oz / 250 ml) thick coconut milk (cream)
2 teaspoons sugar
pinch of salt
6 slices honeydew melon, chilled
1 tablespoon crème de menthe
6 mint sprigs

Pour the coconut milk into a saucepan and bring to the boil. Simmer gently for 25 minutes until well reduced, add sugar and salt, remove from heat and leave to cool. Place in the refrigerator to chill.

Cut skin from each slice of melon in a single strip, set the skin on a dessert plate and position the slice of melon slightly askew on the skin. Sprinkle a few drops of crème de menthe over each melon. Decorate with a sprig of mint. Serve with the reduced coconut milk.

A THAI LUNCH

Serves 6

Scallops Broiled on Skewers with Fried Onion and Peanut Dressing

Red Curry Paste

Minted Chicken Salad

Beef and Long Bean Curry

Sticky Rice with Jackfruit or Mango

Few Thai meals exclude seafood and in this menu I have included skewered scallops served in a traditional style with rice vermicelli and herbs, to fold into little lettuce parcels. The dressing of fried peanuts, onion and chili offers a textural contrast to the tender scallops.

The minted chicken salad has a citrus tang to prepare the palate for the fiery curry. This is a classic Thai red curry, acquiring its name from the heavy use of dried red chilies. You should offer plenty of plain white long grain rice with this dish.

I have chosen one of my favorite desserts to complete the meal. The soothing sticky rice pudding in a coconut milk sauce would be served with jackfruit segments or mango in Thailand, but you may choose another fruit or a fruit salad to suit the season.

Plan well and cook in advance so you can relax. You will need to presoak the rice for the dessert. The curry can be cooked the day before and the chicken early in the morning. The scallops can be skewered in readiness, although do not marinate for more than an hour or the seasonings will overshadow the seafood.

A day or two ahead, make the red curry paste, or try a bottled Thai red curry paste.

SCALLOPS BROILED ON SKEWERS WITH FRIED ONION AND
PEANUT DRESSING

Scallops Broiled on Skewers with Fried Onion and Peanut Dressing

▲▲▲▲▲▲

*Allow 6 scallops per person, selecting those with
their coral*
¾ inch (2 cm) piece fresh ginger
1 clove garlic
1 lemon grass stalk, white part only
1 teaspoon ground coriander
¼ teaspoon black pepper
½ cup vegetable oil
1 tablespoon peanuts
2 scallions (spring onions), finely chopped
½ fresh red chili pepper, seeded
fine bamboo skewers
12 small lettuce cups
1 cup cooked rice vermicelli
*sprigs of fresh mint, sweet basil or
fresh coriander*

Thread three scallops onto each skewer. Place
them in a flat dish.

Combine the ginger, garlic, lemon grass,
coriander, pepper and 3 tablespoons vegetable oil
in a blender, food processor or mortar and grind
to a smooth paste. Spread over the scallops, cover
with plastic wrap and refrigerate for 1 hour to
absorb the seasonings.

Heat charcoal for a small broiler (grill). When
it is glowing, cover with the mesh grid, which has
been brushed with oil to prevent the scallops
sticking.

In a small saucepan heat the remaining oil and
fry the peanuts until golden, retrieve with a
slotted spoon and chop finely. Fry the scallions
and chili, remove and stir in the peanuts.
Leave to cool.

Broil (grill) scallops quickly on each side; they
should be cooked until just crisp in texture. Dip
into the scallion sauce.

To serve, place a portion of rice vermicelli
and a few fresh herbs on each lettuce leaf.
Remove scallops from skewers, place in the
lettuce and roll up. Serve with Thai fish and
chili sauces.

Red Curry Paste

▲▲▲▲▲▲

10 dried red chili peppers, soaked
*1 tablespoon shredded dried Kaffir lime skin,
soaked*
4 dried Kaffir lime leaves, soaked
2 lemon grass stalks, trimmed and chopped
3 tablespoons fresh coriander roots and stems
1½ inch (4 cm) piece fresh ginger
8 cloves garlic, peeled
1 medium onion, peeled and roughly chopped
1½ teaspoons shrimp paste
1 tablespoon palm or brown sugar
2 tablespoons fish sauce

Drain the soaked ingredients. Place them all in a food processor or mortar and grind to a smooth paste, adding a little water if required. If preparing in advance, spoon into a sealed container, smooth the surface and cover with a film of vegetable oil. It can be refrigerated for several weeks.

Minted Chicken Salad

▲▲▲▲▲▲

1 lb (500 g) boneless, skinless chicken breasts
1 large red salad (Spanish) onion
1 medium cucumber
½ red pepper (capsicum)
2 scallions (spring onions), chopped
1 cup loosely packed fresh mint leaves
¼ cup loosely packed sweet basil or coriander leaves

1 tablespoon tamari soy sauce
1½ tablespoons Thai fish sauce
2 tablespoons lime juice
2 cloves garlic, chopped finely
3 teaspoons sugar
1 teaspoon dried chili flakes

Cut the chicken into small cubes. Heat a non-stick pan and cook the chicken on moderate heat without oil until it turns white and is barely cooked through, remove and leave to cool.

Peel and finely slice the onion and cucumber. Trim and shred the red pepper. Combine the salad ingredients in a large bowl.

Combine the sauces, lime juice, garlic, sugar and chili flakes in a screw-top jar. Shake vigorously to combine, pour over the salad, toss and serve.

MINTED CHICKEN SALAD

BEEF AND LONG BEAN CURRY

Beef and Long Bean Curry

▲▲▲▲▲▲

3 lb (1½ kg) braising beef (flank, shin, round etc.)
4 cups (32 fl oz / 1 l) thin coconut milk
1 large onion, roughly chopped
2 tablespoons vegetable oil
1 tablespoon coriander seeds
3-4 tablespoons red curry paste, or use commercially prepared red curry paste according to directions
¾ lb (375 g) Chinese long (snake) beans or green beans
salt, pepper and lime juice
fresh coriander sprigs
1 fresh red chili, seeded and shredded

Cut the beef into 1¼ inch (3 cm) cubes and place in a stewpan with the coconut milk. Bring to the boil and simmer for 10 minutes, then drain, reserving the coconut milk.

Heat the oil in the same pan and sauté the onion until lightly browned, add the curry paste and cook, stirring continually, for about 5 minutes. Pour in the coconut milk and bring almost to the boil, reduce heat and allow the sauce to simmer for about 25 minutes.

In the meantime, toast the coriander seeds in a pan without oil, or in a hot oven, then grind finely. Add to the sauce.

Return the meat and simmer, covered, for 1 hour. It may be necessary to add a little more liquid (either water or coconut milk) as the dish should have a generous amount of sauce.

Top and tail the beans and cut into 2 inch (5 cm) lengths. Add to the curry and cook until beans and meat are tender. Season to taste with salt and pepper, and add a dash of lime juice to heighten the taste.

Transfer to a serving dish and garnish with the coriander and chili shreds. Serve with fragrant Thai Jasmine rice, or an alternate, aromatic, long-grain rice such as Basmati cooked by the absorption method and decorated with sprigs of fresh herbs.

Sticky Rice with Jackfruit or Mango

▲▲▲▲▲▲

1½ cups glutinous white rice, soaked overnight
14 fl oz (440 ml) can thick coconut
milk (cream)
½ teaspoon salt
¼ cup crumbled palm or demerara sugar
1 large can jackfruit segments or fresh mango

Drain the rice, rinse with cold water and drain again. Place in a medium-sized heavy saucepan and add 1½ cups water. Bring to the boil, then reduce heat to low and cook with the pan tightly covered, until the rice is tender and the liquid absorbed.

Separately, boil the coconut milk with salt until reduced by half. And in another pan simmer the sugar with 1 tablespoon water to make a syrup. Allow coconut milk and syrup to cool.

To assemble the dessert, transfer the rice to an oiled ring tin and press in firmly, allow to cool before removing onto a serving plate. Fill the middle with drained jackfruit pieces and serve the coconut milk and syrup separately.

STICKY RICE WITH JACKFRUIT OR MANGO

DINNER IN JAVA

Serves 6

Little Fish Parcels

Hot Chili Eggs

Javanese Chicken

Crisp-fried Onion

Chili Sambal

Coconut Sago Pudding

Enjoy an evening of Javanese food, the Indonesian island where dishes hot with chilies are adored. Generally, the first course at an Indonesian dinner will be a vegetable, noodle or seafood soup, or tasty snack foods, like the fish parcels I have chosen. To follow these delicacies, with their nutty, fiery-hot coating of coconut, I have selected two main dishes. The eggs have a complex and assertive sauce which brings together many standard Indonesian seasonings – lemon grass, tamarind, turmeric, pungent compressed shrimp paste, and sweet soy sauce. While the chicken balances the menu with a sweeter, hot but creamy sauce.

Plain white rice is the usual accompaniment to bold Indonesian dishes, but I enjoy the soothing qualities of rice cooked in coconut milk when I'm eating chili-hot foods. Dress up a dish with finely shredded egg crepe and fresh coriander. Crisp-fried onions are also used as a garnish for many Indonesian dishes. They can be made in advance and stored in a screwtop jar.

Complement these intriguing tastes with a *sambal,* and a side dish of onion rings marinated in vinegar with salt and sugar, mixed with pineapple wedges and a sprinkle of chili flakes and chopped mint. Sago pudding is soothing and therefore the perfect way to finish this meal.

LITTLE FISH PARCELS

Little Fish Parcels

▲▲▲▲▲▲

In Indonesia these slivers of fish with their chili-coconut coating are so fiercely hot you are virtually rendered speechless with every bite. These are much safer! They look and taste wonderful roasted in banana leaves, however aluminum foil gives good results and they can be cooked in a hot oven for convenience. If you like, make them in advance and freeze or refrigerate until needed.

1 lb (500 g) boneless, skinless white fish
1 tablespoon coriander seeds
2 dried red chili peppers, soaked in hot water
2 scallions (spring onions), trimmed and sliced
1 lemon grass stalk, trimmed and chopped

¾ inch (2 cm) piece fresh ginger
2 cloves garlic
½ teaspoon blachan (compressed shrimp paste)
12 kemiri (candlenuts) or macadamia nuts
1⅓ cups (4 oz / 120 g) finely shredded
(desiccated) coconut
24 pieces young banana leaf or aluminum foil,
each 5 inch (12.5 cm) square
vegetable oil
toothpicks

Cut the fish into very thin slivers and set to one side.

Roast the coriander seeds in a dry pan on a moderately high heat until they are aromatic and beginning to pop. Transfer to a mortar or spice grinder and grind to a fine powder.

Drain chilies, deseed and place in a food processor. Add onions, lemon grass, ginger, garlic, shrimp paste and nuts and process to a smooth paste. Add coriander, coconut and enough vegetable oil to make the paste moist. Process until thoroughly blended.

Brush with oil one side of each piece of banana leaf or aluminum foil. Place two teaspoons of the coconut mixture in the middle of each and press on a piece of fish, cover with the remaining paste.

Fold into a rectangular parcel, securing the ends with toothpicks. Cook over gently glowing charcoal, in a hot oven or under a moderately hot broiler (grill) until the banana leaf is charred at the edges and the fish cooked through.

Hot Chili Eggs

▲▲▲▲▲▲

8 large chicken or duck eggs, hard-boiled
oil for deep-frying
1 large onion, chopped very finely
3 cloves garlic, chopped finely
1 teaspoon grated fresh ginger
1 teaspoon blachan (compressed shrimp paste)
2-3 teaspoons sambal ulek or other chili paste

1 lemon grass stalk, trimmed and chopped
1 teaspoon tamarind concentrate, or 2 teaspoons tamarind pulp
1½ teaspoons brown sugar
1 tablespoon sweet dark soy sauce
½ teaspoon ground turmeric
salt and pepper
1 fresh red chili, seeded and shredded
chopped fresh coriander

Peel the eggs. Heat the oil in a deep pan and fry the eggs until the surface is golden brown and slightly bubbled, remove from the oil and drain on absorbent paper.

Transfer 2 tablespoons of the oil to a sauté pan and sauté the onion until well browned. Add garlic, ginger and shrimp paste and sauté for 2-3 minutes, then add the remaining ingredients except fresh chili and coriander and cook for 1 minute, stirring well. Add ½ cup water and bring to the boil, simmer for 2 minutes. At this point, the sauce can be blended smoothly if preferred.

Halve the eggs lengthwise and place in the sauce. Cook gently for 5 minutes, turning several times. Serve garnished with the chili and coriander.

HOT CHILI EGGS

JAVANESE CHICKEN

Javanese Chicken

▲▲▲▲▲▲

3 lb (1½ kg) chicken portions
2 cups (16 fl oz / 500 ml) vegetable oil
2 large onions, sliced finely
4 cloves garlic, chopped finely
1¼ inch (3 cm) piece fresh ginger, chopped finely
1⅓ teaspoons blachan (shrimp paste)
2 tablespoons sweet soy sauce
1 tablespoon crumbled palm or demerara sugar
2–3 fresh red chilies, seeded and sliced
4 medium tomatoes, seeded and chopped
1 cup (8 fl oz / 250 ml) thick coconut
milk (cream)
salt and pepper

Cut the chicken into 2½ inch (5 cm) pieces and fry in the oil until golden on the surface. Remove and drain, pour off all but 2 tablespoons of the oil and sauté the onion until golden.

Add garlic, ginger and shrimp paste and sauté briefly. Return the chicken, add the soy sauce and sugar and 1 cup water. Cover and cook for 10 minutes. Add chili and tomatoes and continue to cook on low heat until the chicken is just tender.

Add coconut milk and seasonings to taste, simmer briefly and serve.

Crisp-fried Onion

▲▲▲▲▲▲

Indonesian cooks prefer to use small red shallot bulbs for this recipe, but you can use small to medium brown (yellow) onions. Heat a pan with 3–4 cups vegetable oil. Peel, halve and very finely slice twenty or so shallots or several medium-sized onions. Fry them in the oil until they are a deep golden brown and are making a crisp, rustling sound when lifted from the oil. Once they begin to brown deeply it is a matter of seconds before they burn, so be vigilant and remove them individually as they are ready. Drain well on absorbent paper and leave to cool. They can be stored in an airtight jar in the refrigerator for several months.

Chili Sambal

▲▲▲▲▲▲

2 tablespoons sambal ulek or other chili paste
1 small onion, grated and drained
2 cloves garlic, mashed
2 tablespoons crumbled palm or dark brown sugar
2 tablespoons vinegar
½ cup (4 fl oz / 125 ml) water
salt to taste
2 tablespoons roasted peanuts, chopped

Place the ingredients, except peanuts, in a small saucepan and bring to the boil. Simmer until slightly reduced and syrupy.

Cool and transfer to a small screwtop jar to store. Stir in peanuts before serving.

Coconut Sago Pudding

▲▲▲▲▲▲

¾ cup (4 oz / 125 g) sago
3 cups (24 fl oz / 750 ml) thin coconut milk
1 bruised pandan leaf (optional)
½ cup (4 oz / 125 g) sugar

Boil the ingredients together for about 12 minutes until sago is transparent. Discard leaf, if used. Allow the dessert to cool before serving in small glass bowls.

COCONUT SAGO PUDDING

A NIGHT IN SINGAPORE

Serves 6

*Crispy Penang Chicken Wings with
Sweet Pickled Cucumber*

Singapore Chili Crab

Creamy Lamb Curry

Burbur Cha Cha

Singaporean food is a blending of three cultures – Chinese, Indian and Malay. Often a meal, or even a single dish, will contain elements of all three. You will find stir-fries seasoned with soy sauce and ginger, richly spiced curries, bright yellow turmeric and coconut milk sauces fiery with chilies, clear soups and plenty of rice.

I like to balance tastes and textures in a meal. The chicken wings are crunchy crisp, their dipping sauce and the sweet pickle that accompanies them offsetting their subtle taste. Singapore Chili Crab is boldly seasoned, so I have chosen a gently spiced creamy curry to accompany it. Offer steamed white rice, and prepare a green salad or a plate of sliced tomatoes and cucumber dressed with a profusion of chopped fresh herbs.

The dessert is Burbur Cha Cha, a typical Singaporean dessert popular for casual meals. It is soothing and refreshing, ideal to serve after a highly seasoned meal.

Serve a crisp light white wine or champagne, along with soda or mineral water with slivers of fresh lime. Cold beer or tropical fruit juices combined with carbonated drinks, and perhaps a splash of vermouth or white rum, make a deliciously refreshing punch to serve over crushed ice.

Crispy Penang Chicken Wings with Sweet Pickled Cucumber

▲▲▲▲▲▲

18 chicken wings (you will require only the central portion containing two thin bones, the remainder can be used in another recipe or simmered for stock)
1 tablespoon fresh ginger, grated
2 teaspoons garlic, crushed
2 teaspoons chili sauce
1¼ teaspoons ground turmeric
2 teaspoons sugar
2 tablespoons lime juice
¾ cup (6 fl oz / 180 ml) thick coconut milk (cream)
oil for deep frying
krupuk (peanut crisps)
¼ cup (2 fl oz / 60 ml) Worcestershire sauce
2 teaspoons hot English mustard
sugar and lime juice to taste

CRISPY PENANG CHICKEN WINGS WITH SWEET PICKLED CUCUMBER

Serve in several small dishes and offer small dishes of sweet pickled cucumber as well. You may buy bottled or canned pickles, or make your own.

To prepare the chicken wings, separate the upper and lower joints and set aside for separate use. Place wings in a wide shallow dish.

Place the ginger and garlic in a small piece of cloth, and squeeze the contents over a mixing bowl to extract their juices. Add the chili sauce, turmeric, sugar and lime juice and mix well, then stir in the coconut milk.

Pour the marinade over the wings, cover with plastic wrap and marinate for at least 6 hours, or overnight.

Drain the wings well and pat dry with paper towels. Heat deep oil for frying and fry the wings until crisp and golden on the surface. Drain well. Fry the krupuk until they float to the surface and expand, remove and drain well. Arrange wings and krupuk on a platter.

Whisk the Worcestershire sauce and mustard together, adding sugar and lime juice to taste.

Sweet Pickled Cucumber

▲▲▲▲▲▲

2 small cucumbers
2 teaspoons salt
2 tablespoons fine white sugar
2½ tablespoons white vinegar

Peel the cucumbers, cut in halves lengthwise and use a teaspoon or melon baller to remove the central fibrous section and seeds. Slice thinly.

Place in a dish and sprinkle the salt evenly over, leave for 15 minutes. Lightly 'knead' the cucumber with the fingers to soften it, add the other ingredients and set aside for 30 minutes. Drain, and if preferred, rinse before serving.

Singapore Chili Crab

▲▲▲▲▲▲

2-3 large crabs with heavy pincers
2 medium onions
3-4 tablespoons vegetable oil
3 cloves garlic, finely chopped
1½ inch (4 cm) piece fresh ginger, finely chopped
1 tablespoon sambal ulek or other chili paste
2 teaspoons tamarind concentrate
2½ tablespoons sugar
¼ cup (2 fl oz / 60 ml) tomato ketchup
¾ cup (6 fl oz / 180 ml) fish stock or water
1 tablespoon cornstarch (cornflour)
salt and cracked black pepper
6 scallions (spring onions), chopped
1-2 tablespoons fresh coriander, chopped
(optional)
1 fresh red chili pepper, seeded and
chopped finely

Thoroughly wash the crabs to remove any mud. Place in a large pan of lightly salted water to boil for 5 minutes, remove and leave to cool.

Lift the back shell from each crab and remove all inedible parts. Rinse again. Remove pincers and crack the hard shell with a hammer or heavy pestle to allow access. Very large pincers may be cut in half with a heavy cleaver. Use the cleaver also to divide the body into six pieces, each with a leg attached.

Cut top and base from onions and slice vertically into narrow wedges. In a large wok or sauté pan, heat the oil and stir-fry the onions until they begin to soften. Add garlic and ginger and stir-fry briefly. Add the crabs and stir-fry on high heat for about 4 minutes.

Add the tamarind, chili paste, sugar and ketchup, and the stock mixed with cornstarch and bring to a boil, stirring to thicken. Stir in onions and cook briefly.

Serve garnished with coriander and chili.

SINGAPORE CHILI CRAB

CREAMY LAMB CURRY

Creamy Lamb Curry

▲▲▲▲▲▲

2 lb (1 kg) boneless lamb
2 tablespoons vegetable oil
2 medium-sized onions, chopped
3 cloves garlic, finely chopped
2-3 tablespoons mild curry powder
1½ teaspoons salt
½ teaspoon cracked black pepper
2 cups (16 fl oz / 500 ml) thin coconut milk
2 large potatoes
1 cup (180 g / 6 oz) fresh or frozen peas
¾ cup (6 fl oz / 180 ml) thick coconut milk (cream)
3 eggs, hard-boiled
2 tablespoons toasted almonds
chopped fresh mint or coriander

Cut the lamb into 1¼ inch (3 cm) cubes and brown in the oil in a large frying pan. Remove and keep warm. Brown the onions in the oil, then add the garlic and cook briefly. Add curry powder and stir over moderate heat for 2 minutes.

Return the lamb, add seasonings and thin coconut milk with 1 cup (8 fl oz / 250 ml) water. Bring to the boil, reduce heat and simmer with the pan partially covered, for 45 minutes.

Peel and cube the potatoes. Add potatoes and peas to the curry and cook until vegetables and meat are tender (if using frozen peas, add when potatoes are almost cooked). Stir in thick coconut milk and halved eggs and heat through. Add almonds and check seasoning.

Serve over rice, garnished with the fresh herbs.

Burbur Cha Cha

▲▲▲▲▲▲

2½ oz (75 g) arrowroot or green mung bean flour
few drops food coloring
1 medium-sized yellow sweet potato
3 cups (24 fl oz / 750 ml) coconut milk
½ cup (2½ oz / 75 g) crumbled palm **or**
demerara sugar
shaved ice

Boil the flour with 1½ cups water until it thickens and becomes transparent; divide into two portions and tint one green and the other pink. Press the batter through the holes of a colander placed over a dish of ice-water. The batter will form into little bean shapes. Drain.

Peel the potato and slice thickly. Boil in lighty salted water until tender, drain, and cut into small dice. Boil the coconut milk with about ¾ teaspoon salt until slightly reduced. Cool.

In a small saucepan make a syrup by boiling the sugar with 3 tablespoons water until slightly thickened. Cool.

To assemble the dessert half-fill dessert dishes with shaved ice. Divide the ingredients among the dishes and serve.

BURBUR CHA CHA

DIM SUM BRUNCH

Serves 8

Steamed Beefballs

Chicken Salad with Sesame and Mustard Sauces

Sesame Shrimp Toast

Garlic Chive Dumplings

Won Ton Knots

Chinese Green Vegetables with Oyster Sauce

Sweet and Sour Sauce

Even after two decades of frequent Chinese *yum cha* brunches, I still rate this mode of eating one of my best. The tiny dumplings, buns and rolls called *dim sum* have their own special appeal, and guests will be impressed to find you have prepared them yourself. You could easily expand this menu for a larger group by supplementing a pre-made pack or two.

The Chinese place enormous importance on the careful choice of dishes for a meal. The menu should have balance and contrast, offsetting a sweet taste with tart, bland with bold, crisp with smooth. These *dim sum* dishes reflect that philosophy. The meatballs are smoothly textured and subtle in taste, the duo of nutty and piquant sauces enhance the blandness of the chicken and vermicelli. Crispness comes with the won tons and the shrimp toast and strong, fresh tastes are found in the garlic chive dumplings. Many *dim sum* restaurants now offer freshly cooked Chinese green vegetables, bathed in oyster sauce, so I have decided to add these to my menu.

Serve these dishes one or two at a time. Soy

sauce, a hot chili and a fiery mustard, served in small dishes for dipping, suit the steamed dishes, and offer the sweet and sour sauce with the shrimp toast and won ton knots.

Fragrant Chinese jasmine teas or the darker *bo lay* are an obvious beverage choice, but when alcoholic drinks seem appropriate, serve a good quality brandy spritzed with soda, on ice.

Steamed Beefballs

▲▲▲▲▲▲

1 lb (500 g) lean minced (ground) beef
¼ cup (2 fl oz / 125 ml) water
3 tablespoons vegetable oil
1 clove garlic, crushed
1 teaspoon lemon peel, finely grated

¾ teaspoon bicarbonate of soda
½ teaspoon salt
2 teaspoons sugar
1 teaspoon sesame oil
1½ oz (45 g) rice vermicelli, soaked
1 tablespoon soy sauce

In a food processor combine all the ingredients, except rice vermicelli and soy sauce. Process to a smooth and sticky paste.

Drain the vermicelli and use kitchen scissors to snip it into short lengths. Arrange on a heat-resistant plate which will fit inside a large steamer. Pour on the soy sauce.

Use wet or oiled hands to form the mixture into walnut-sized balls and arrange on the plate. Set in a steamer over simmering water and steam for approximately 10 minutes. These beefballs are delicious served with hot mustard.

STEAMED BEEFBALLS

CHICKEN SALAD WITH SESAME AND MUSTARD SAUCES

Chicken Salad with Sesame and Mustard Sauces

▲▲▲▲▲▲

1 lb (500 g) cooked boneless chicken
3 oz (90 g) rice vermicelli or vermicelli sheets, soaked
2 teaspoons Chinese chili oil
3 scallions (spring onions), trimmed and shredded
2-3 sprigs fresh coriander

Sesame Sauce:

3 tablespoons sesame paste (tahini)
3 teaspoons sesame oil
1 tablespoon vegetable oil
lemon juice or white vinegar
sugar, salt and pepper

Mustard Sauce:

2 tablespoons hot mustard powder
1 tablespoon vegetable oil

Tear the chicken into shreds. Drain the vermicelli and snip into short lengths, or roll and shred the sheets. Mix chicken and vermicelli together and arrange on a serving plate, sprinkle with the chili oil and scallions and garnish with coriander.

In a small bowl, combine the ingredients for sesame sauce, adding lemon juice or vinegar and sugar, salt and pepper to taste. Add enough cold water to make a smooth sauce the consistency of thick cream. Pour into a small dip dish for each guest.

Whisk the mustard powder with water and oil to make the second sauce. Serve in a small dish with a spoon.

SESAME SHRIMP TOAST

Sesame Shrimp Toast

▲▲▲▲▲▲

6 slices white bread, preferably 2 days old
8 oz (250 g) fresh shrimp
1 oz (30 g) pork fat
6 water-chestnuts, drained
2 scallions (spring onions), trimmed
1 teaspoon salt
⅓ teaspoon white pepper
1 tablespoon yellow rice wine
1 large egg white, lightly beaten
2 tablespoons cornstarch (cornflour)
½ cup (2½ oz / 75 g) white sesame seeds
oil for deep-frying

Trim bread crusts and cut each piece into four triangles.

Shell and rinse the shrimp and place on a cutting board. Bat with the side of a cleaver blade to reduce to a pulp. Cut the pork fat, water-chestnuts and scallions very finely, mix with the shrimp and add the seasonings, wine, egg white and cornstarch, mixing to a smooth paste.

Spread a portion of filling on each piece of bread, making it thick in the middle and tapering off at the edges. Sprinkle generously with sesame seeds, pressing them on lightly.

Heat deep oil and fry the toasts, filling downward, until golden, turn and briefly cook the bread side. Remove on a slotted spoon and drain thoroughly. Serve hot, with a sweet chili or sweet and sour sauce.

Garlic Chive Dumplings

▲▲▲▲▲▲

1 pack (20-24 pieces) won ton skins (wrappers)
5 dried black mushrooms
18 oz (550 g) coarsely minced (ground) pork
2 oz (50 g) bamboo shoots, drained and finely chopped
¾ cup loosely packed chopped garlic chives
2 tablespoons light soy sauce
1 teaspoon sugar
salt and white pepper
cornstarch (cornflour)
vegetable oil

Defrost won ton skins, if frozen, under a cloth to prevent them drying out.

Drain the mushrooms and remove stems, chop caps finely. Combine with the pork, finely chopped bamboo shoots and garlic chives and the seasonings.

Place a portion of the filling in the centre of each skin bring the corners in together to form square parcels.

In a small saucepan make a paste of cornstarch flour and water, boiling it until it becomes translucent. Use to seal the dumplings.

Place in a steamer and steam for 15 minutes, remove and set aside for 10 minutes to allow the skins to dry.

Heat a nonstick pan and add a film of oil. Fry the dumplings briefly on both sides. Serve with a hot chili sauce.

GARLIC CHIVE DUMPLINGS

Won Ton Knots

▲▲▲▲▲▲

12 small (4 inch / 10 cm) square egg roll
(spring roll) skins, or squares of presoaked
beancurd skin
36 small shelled fresh shrimp
2 teaspoons yellow rice wine
½ teaspoon salt
¼ teaspoon white pepper
1 tablespoon very finely chopped scallion
(spring onion)
1½ teaspoons grated fresh ginger
oil for deep frying
extra salt
2 tablespoons cornstarch (cornflour)

If frozen, thaw the skins under a cloth to prevent them drying out.

In a mixing bowl combine the remaining ingredients, except frying oil, extra salt and cornstarch, and set aside for 15 minutes.

Make a paste for sealing the knots by boiling the cornstarch with ½ cup water until it turns thick and somewhat transparent.

To assemble the knots, place three shrimp in the middle of each skin and bunch the skin around it. You should have small bundles pinched at the top. Brush a little of the paste along the edges and pinch together to seal.

Heat deep oil and fry the won tons, several at a time, until crisp and golden. Drain well, sprinkle with extra salt and serve while still very hot, with a sweet and sour sauce.

CHINESE GREEN VEGETABLES WITH OYSTER SAUCE

Chinese Green Vegetables with Oyster Sauce

▲▲▲▲▲▲

1 lb (500 g) Chinese green vegetables or broccoli
2-3 tablespoons vegetable oil
1 teaspoon sugar
2 tablespoons oyster sauce

Cut the vegetable stems into 2½ inch (6 cm) lengths.

Heat the oil in a wok or sauté pan with a lid. Add vegetables and stir-fry for 2 minutes, then add 3 tablespoons water, cover pan and cook on medium-high heat, shaking the pan occasionally to turn the vegetables, until the liquid evaporates.

Add sugar and half the oyster sauce, close pan again and cook gently for 1 minute, then transfer to a serving dish and pour on the remaining sauce.

Sweet and Sour Sauce

▲▲▲▲▲▲

½ cup (4 fl oz / 125 ml) white vinegar
½ cup (3½ oz / 110 g) white sugar
¼ cup (2 fl oz / 60 ml) tomato ketchup
1 cup (8 fl oz / 250 ml) water
1¼ tablespoons cornstarch (cornflour)
1 teaspoon grated fresh ginger
2 teaspoons Chinese pickles, finely shredded
(optional)

Combine the ingredients in a saucepan, bring to the boil and then reduce heat and stir the sauce until it thickens and turns slightly translucent.

Cool and pour into small dishes to serve. It can be refrigerated for a week or two, if required.

A VIETNAMESE CELEBRATION

Serves 6

Broiled (Grilled) Pork Meatballs with Salad Platter

Chicken with Lemon Grass and Chili

Steamed, Stuffed Whole Fish

Green Sticky Rice with Peanuts and Coconut

Vietnamese cooking employs subtle nuances of taste in the tradition of southern China, in contrast to the more robust tastes of other Asian countries. They add seasoning highlights with fiery chili-based sauces, and splash on the pungent fish sauce they call *nuoc mam*. Fresh enhancements come from the profusion of salad vegetables and the lemony and minty herbs that are served with most meals and are even stirred into bowls of rice vermicelli soup.

In this menu, the salad platter is served as the first course with broiled (grilled) pork meatballs, which are wrapped in moistened rice paper sheets. To follow I offset the lemon and chili tang of the chicken dish with the more earthy, Chinese character of the fish with its mushroom and bamboo shoots stuffing. They would be served at the same time, with plain white rice.

Chinese tea, served warm in tumblers, or a refreshing home-made limeade of freshly squeezed lime juice sweetened with sugar syrup over ice, would traditionally accompany a Vietnamese meal. Serve a crisp, white wine with a hint of sweetness, or a rosé.

BROILED (GRILLED) PORK MEATBALLS WITH SALAD PLATTER

Broiled (Grilled) Pork Meatballs with Salad Platter

▲▲▲▲▲▲

Broiling these over glowing charcoal gives the tastiest results. If you have access to a small broiler (grill), of the type used for cooking satay, or an hibachi, either would be ideal. Heat the charcoal in advance so that it glows a dull-red when cooking begins.

1 lb (500 g) lean pork, diced
2 oz (60 g) pork fat, diced
1½ oz (45 g) canned water-chestnuts, drained
1 scallion (spring onion), chopped roughly
2 teaspoons Vietnamese fish sauce
½ teaspoon salt
¼ teaspoon white pepper

2 tablespoons vegetable oil
12 thin bamboo skewers, soaked in oil
12 x 8 inch (20 cm) dried banh trang rice paper sheets
12 small lettuce leaves
1 medium carrot
3 oz (90 g) fresh beansprouts
fresh mint and basil leaves
Chinese barbecue sauce

Place the pork, pork fat, water-chestnuts and scallions in a food processor and grind them finely. Add fish sauce, salt and pepper and 1 tablespoon oil and process to a smooth paste.

Form into small balls and thread several onto each skewer. Cook under a broiler (grill) or over glowing charcoal, until well browned on the surface and tender inside.

Dip the rice papers into cold water to soften, drain well and arrange on a wide platter with the washed and dried lettuce leaves. Coarsely grate the carrot, arrange on the plate with beansprouts and herbs. Serve the sauce in several small dishes for dipping.

To eat, cut the meatballs in half and remove from the skewers. Serve with the platter. Place a piece of lettuce on a sheet of rice paper. Dip a few pieces of meatball in the sauce, place on the lettuce, add carrot, beansprouts and a few herbs, roll up to eat.

Chicken with Lemon Grass and Chili

▲▲▲▲▲▲

1½ lb (750 g) chicken (thigh portions)
1 tablespoon Vietnamese fish sauce
salt and white pepper
2 lemon grass stalks, trimmed
2 scallions (spring onions), trimmed
3 tablespoons vegetable oil
2 fresh red chilies, seeded and sliced
1 teaspoon crumbled palm or brown sugar

Cut the chicken portions in half, through the bone. Use a sharp skewer to prick the chicken, to allow seasonings to penetrate. Place in a dish and pour on the fish sauce, sprinkle on seasonings and leave for 15 minutes.

Very finely chop the lemon grass and scallions. Heat the oil in a large sauté pan or a wok and brown the chicken evenly. Add the lemon grass and onions and 1 cup water. Cover and cook until the chicken is almost tender, about 15 minutes, turning several times. Add the chilies and sugar and cook another 5-7 minutes. The liquid should evaporate, leaving the chicken free of sauce. Serve over rice.

CHICKEN WITH LEMON GRASS AND CHILI

Steamed, Stuffed Whole Fish

▲▲▲▲▲▲

1 large sea bass, snapper, or suitable reef fish,
weighing at least 2 lbs (1 kg)
3 dried black mushrooms, soaked
½ oz (15 g) dried black fungus (wood ears),
soaked
2 scallions (spring onions), trimmed
1½ oz (45 g) canned bamboo shoots, drained
1½ oz (45 g) coarsely minced (ground) pork or
chicken
1 oz (30 g) bean thread vermicelli, soaked
2 teaspoons brown sugar
2 tablespoons dark soy sauce
black pepper
1¼ inch (3 cm) piece fresh ginger, very finely
shredded
2 tablespoons vegetable oil

Clean and scale the fish and make several deep slashes, at even intervals, diagonally across each side.

Drain soaked fungus, trim mushroom stems. Very finely shred all of the vegetables and cut the vermicelli into 2 inch (4 cm) lengths. Mix with the sugar and half the soy, and stuff into the fish. Secure the opening with a thin bamboo skewer.

Place the fish on a platter which will fit inside a large steamer (or improvise with a rack inside a wok). Pour on remaining soy and sprinkle on pepper evenly. Arrange ginger over the fish and pour on the oil. Place in the steamer and steam over simmering water for about 20 minutes.

Test the fish at the thickest part. If the flesh parts easily, it is done. Remove from the heat and stand in the steamer for 3-4 minutes before taking directly to the table on its plate with steamed white rice.

STEAMED, STUFFED WHOLE FISH

GREEN STICKY RICE WITH PEANUTS AND COCONUT

Green Sticky Rice with Peanuts and Coconut

▲▲▲▲▲▲

*9 oz (280 g) glutinous rice, presoaked for
5-6 hours
2 teaspoons salt
1 pandan leaf or ⅓ teaspoon green food coloring
1 cup (8 fl oz / 250 ml) coconut milk
¼ cup shredded coconut
1 tablespoon vegetable oil
1 tablespoon salted peanuts, skinned
2-3 teaspoons palm or brown sugar*

Place the drained rice, salt, pandan leaf or food coloring, coconut milk and 2 cups water in a saucepan and bring to the boil. Reduce heat and simmer until the rice is tender and has absorbed the liquid. Discard pandan leaf.

Brush six dessert tins or Chinese rice bowls with oil. Press the rice into the tins and set aside to firm up.

Remove onto plates, decorate each with shredded coconut. In a small pan, sauté the peanuts in the oil until golden, add the sugar and cook until it begins to caramelize. Pour a portion over the top of each dessert. Serve.

VEGETARIAN JAPANESE

Serves 6

Miso Shiru Soup

Eggplant (Aubergine) in Miso Sauce

Nimono of Turnip and Carrot

Pressed Sushi Rice

Tempura of Green Beans, Pumpkin and Peppers

Japanese cooks rely to a large extent on soy beans when vegetables feature in a meal. They come in many forms – soft *tofu* (beancurd) and fermented *tempeh* and its derivatives. Seaweed, too, plays an important role in Japanese cuisine. Tender lobeleaf seaweed *(wakame)* is consumed as soups and salads. Strands of kelp, called *kombu*, form one of the prime ingredients in their stocks and sauces, and delicate black branches of crisp and crunchy *hijiki* garnish many dishes.

Japanese vegetable dishes are not always strictly vegetarian as *katsuobushi* (shaved, dried, bonito fish) is used in many dishes, as the basic stock for cooking or making sauces.

Serve the first two dishes together, each in its own small dish if you have enough crockery to go around, otherwise in serving dishes at the table.

The soup can be served at any time during the meal, and is traditionally brought to the table in little, covered, lacquered bowls.

The tempura should be cooked immediately before serving, so plan to have a short break in the meal while you return to the kitchen.

MISO SHIRU SOUP

Miso Shiru Soup

▲▲▲▲▲▲

2 x 4 in (10 cm) squares kombu kelp
6 cups (1½ qts / 750 ml) water
2 teaspoons instant dashi granules
6 small dried black mushrooms, soaked
6 tablespoons (5 oz / 150 g) brown or red
miso paste
3 spring (green) onions, trimmed and finely
sliced
1 cup (8 oz / 250 g) soft tofu (beancurd), diced

Rinse and dry the kelp and use a sharp knife to score the surface. Place in a saucepan with the water and dashi and bring just to the boil. Drain mushrooms and remove stems. Cut a cross in the top of each cap, place the mushrooms in the stock and simmer gently for 2 minutes.

While the stock is very gently simmering, stir in 1 tablespoon of the miso and mix well, then slowly stir in the remainder. Do not allow the soup to boil again.

Pour into soup bowls and add the onions and beancurd. Serve at once. The soup should be stirred before drinking.

EGGPLANT (AUBERGINE) IN MISO SAUCE

Eggplant (Aubergine) in Miso Sauce

▲▲▲▲▲▲

1 lb (500 g) large eggplant (aubergine)
2 tablespoons vegetable oil
4 tablespoons (3½ oz / 110 g) red miso
1½ tablespoons white miso
2½ tablespoons mirin (Japanese sherry)
1½ tablespoons sugar
⅓ cup (2½ fl oz / 85 ml) water
¼ teaspoon instant dashi granules
2 small egg yolks
2 teaspoons very finely shredded lime peel

Cut the eggplant into thick slices, about ¾ in (2 cm), and coat with vegetable oil. Place under a hot grill to cook until the eggplant is well softened.

Combine the remaining ingredients, except lime peel, in the top of a double saucepan. Cook slowly, stirring all the time, until it thickens. Spread over the eggplant and return to the grill. Cook until the surface is flecked with brown.

Scatter the lime peel over the top and serve.

Nimono of Turnip and Carrot

▲▲▲▲▲▲

14 oz (450 g) turnip or giant white radish
14 oz (450 g) carrot
2 cups (16 fl oz / 500 ml) water
1 teaspoon instant dashi granules
1 tablespoon mirin (Japanese sherry)
1 tablespoon light soy sauce
1 teaspoon salt

Peel the turnip or radish and the carrot and cut into 1¼ in (3 cm) cubes. Rinse, drain and place in a saucepan.

Add the remaining ingredients, cover and bring to the boil. Reduce heat and simmer very slowly until the vegetables are tender (about 20 minutes). Serve with the sauce.

NIMONO OF TURNIP AND CARROT

PRESSED SUSHI RICE

Pressed Sushi Rice

▲▲▲▲▲▲

½ recipe sushi rice (see Nori Maki Sushi on page 138)
2 eggs, well beaten
2 teaspoons mirin (Japanese sherry)
1 teaspoon vegetable oil
2 sheets nori (compressed seaweed sheets)
½ cup pickled radish or turnip, shredded
2 tablespoons sweet pickled ginger shavings
pepper

Prepare the sushi rice and set aside to cool. Stir mirin into the eggs. Heat a small pan and moisten it with the oil. Pour in the eggs and tilt the pan so the egg forms a very thin crepe. Cook on one side only, then remove.

Hold the nori sheets briefly over a flame to crisp, then remove. Line a square cake tin with aluminum foil and brush with a little vegetable oil. Press half the rice evenly into the tin. Spread the nori and egg over the rice, add the pickles and

sprinkle with pepper. Cover with the remaining rice, pressing firmly. Cover with the aluminum foil and set aside to firm up.

Remove the top foil, turn onto a plate and cut into squares, discarding lower foil. Serve at room temperature.

Tempura of Green Beans, Pumpkin and Peppers

▲▲▲▲▲▲

16 green beans
8 oz (250 g) pumpkin
1 red or yellow pepper (capsicum)
1 large onion
oil for deep-frying
2-3 tablespoons sesame oil

Batter:
2¼ cups (12 oz / 345 g) all-purpose (plain) flour
2 cups (16 fl oz / 500 ml) ice-water
2 large egg yolks

The beans can be left whole or cut in half as preferred. Peel the pumpkin and cut into thin slices. Discard seeds and trim inner ribs from pepper, cut into strips ½ in (1.5 cm) wide or into squares. Peel the onion, cut in half, then into ¼ in (1 cm) thick slices. Press a thin toothpick through the back of each slice of onion so the layers stay together when fried.

Heat the oil in a large pan and add sesame oil. Use a wire strainer lined with absorbent paper when draining the cooked tempura. Use long cooking chopsticks to retrieve fried foods from the oil.

Sift the flour into a large bowl. Beat egg yolks and 1 cup water together, pour over the flour, add the remaining water and quickly and lightly work into the flour. Do not overmix.

Dip the foods piece by piece into the batter

and slide into the oil. Fry until they are golden, floating to the top of the oil, and the vegetables are cooked through. Test by piercing with a skewer. Drain and serve hot with Tempura sauce dip, grated fresh ginger and giant white radish.

Tempura Dip:
½ cup (4 fl oz / 125 ml) water
⅓ teaspoon instant dashi granules
¼ cup (2 fl oz / 60 ml) light or tamari soy sauce
2 tablespoons mirin (Japanese sherry)

2-3 teaspoons sugar
2 tablespoons very finely grated giant white radish (daikon)
1½ teaspoons very finely grated fresh ginger

In a small saucepan bring water to the boil, add dashi, soy, mirin and sugar and boil for 2-3 minutes. Remove and leave to cool. When completely cold, stir in grated radish and ginger and serve in small dishes for dipping.

TEMPURA OF GREEN BEANS, PUMPKIN AND PEPPERS

INDONESIAN RIJSTAFFEL

Serves 8-10

Shrimp and Coconut Fritters

Sweet Braised Pork

*Whole Fish in Spicy Coconut Baked in
Banana Leaves*

Rujak Fruit and Vegetable Salad

Turmeric Rice

Lychee Mousse

Accompaniments:

Fried Shrimp Crisps
Tomato Onion Sambal
Coconut Sambal

A well-balanced Indonesian menu would contain a number of fiery hot curries or heavily seasoned dishes, at least one grilled over charcoal or baked in a banana leaf wrap, like the fish in this menu coated with spicy coconut seasoning. There would be rice, and several side dishes selected to enhance the main food and to add points of interest to the meal.

This is a generous menu, meant for an occasion when you and your friends will want to spend lazy hours lingering over the meal. I have selected a mild-tasting first course of crisp fritters, which should be complemented by a bold chili sauce for dipping. For the main dishes two compatible choices are the sweet and mellow *babi kecap*, with a subtle underlay of chili, and its companion a tender whole fish with a nutty coconut crust. The unusual salad combining vegetables and fruit in a dressing of sweet-sour tastes is cleanly refreshing on the palate. The yellow rice adds a festive note to the meal.

To finish the meal on a pleasing note, the dessert, while not classically Indonesian, introduces a local fruit in a smoothly textured mousse.

The dessert, sambal and salad can all be prepared in advance.

Offer flutes of champagne with guava juice to start and a strong white wine or rosé with a hint of spiciness with the main meal.

Shrimp and Coconut Fritters

▲▲▲▲▲▲

10 oz (300 g) small fresh shrimp
1 cup (5 oz / 150 g) self-raising flour
⅓ cup (1 oz / 30 g) coarsely shredded coconut
½ teaspoon baking powder

1 teaspoon salt
1 large egg
⅓ teaspoon white pepper
2 scallions (spring onions), finely chopped
1 small clove garlic, finely chopped
2 teaspoons dill or fresh coriander, chopped
2 tablespoons vegetable oil

Shell the shrimp and place the shells in a saucepan with 2 cups water. Bring to the boil, simmer for 10 minutes, then strain the liquid into a jug and allow to cool.

Roughly chop the shrimp. Combine shrimp and the remaining ingredients, except oil, in a mixing bowl. Slowly add the cool, reserved liquid to make a creamy batter, adding extra cold water if necessary. Set the batter aside for 25 minutes.

Moisten a frying pan with oil and fry large spoonfuls of the batter until golden brown underneath, turn and cook the other side. The fritters are done when they feel firm in the middle and no uncooked batter exudes when pressed. Keep warm until the remainder are cooked, then serve with a sweet chili sauce dip.

SWEET BRAISED PORK

Sweet Braised Pork

▲▲▲▲▲▲

3 lb (1½ kg) boneless pork *
3 tablespoons vegetable oil
2 medium onions, chopped finely
1½ inch (4 cm) piece fresh ginger, chopped finely
4 cloves garlic, chopped finely
1 tablespoon sambal ulek or other chili paste
¾ cup (6 fl oz / 180 ml) sweet soy sauce
1½ cups (14 fl oz / 375 ml) coconut milk
salt and freshly milled black pepper
* You may use fresh ham (leg or shoulder) or
for a much richer dish use belly pork
(fresh bacon) and skim off excess fat before
serving.

Cut the pork into 1½ inch (4 cm) cubes. Heat the oil in a large skillet or wok and brown the pork in several batches. Transfer meat to a heavy stewpan or casserole. Brown the onion in the same pan, then add the garlic, ginger and sambal ulek and cook for 1-2 minutes.

Pour in the soy sauce and coconut milk and bring almost to the boil. Pour over the pork, then simmer on low heat or bake in a moderate to low oven for 1 hour.

Add seasoning to taste, add a little more liquid if needed - the finished dish should have just a small amount of sauce, and continue to cook until the pork is tender enough to tear with a fork.

Serve with steamed rice which has been decorated with egg shreds, and fresh herbs.

Whole Fish in Spicy Coconut Baked in Banana Leaves

▲▲▲▲▲▲

4 lb (2 kg) sea bass or reef fish
(or 2 smaller fish)
2½ teaspoons tamarind concentrate
1¾ teaspoons salt
½ teaspoon white pepper
1 tablespoon ginger, grated
2 teaspoons ground turmeric
3 teaspoons sambal ulek or other chile paste
1 teaspoon blachan (compressed shrimp paste)
2 teaspoons sugar
8 kemiri (candlenuts), ground
(or use raw cashews)
1 cup (3 oz / 90 g) finely shredded (desiccated)
coconut
½ -¾ cup (4-6 fl oz / 125-180 ml) thick coconut
milk (cream)
vegetable oil
young, soft banana leaves and / or
aluminum foil

Preheat the kettle barbecue according to the instructions, or prepare charcoal in a standard barbecue.

Gut and scale the fish and rinse thoroughly, draining well. Make several deep slashes, diagonally on each side, to allow seasonings to penetrate. Dilute tamarind with a little water and paint over the outside of the fish and in the cavity, season with salt and pepper.

Combine ginger, sambal ulek, turmeric, mashed blachan, sugar, nuts and dry coconut, with enough of the coconut milk to make a thick paste. Cut away the thick, central ribs from banana leaves and brush with oil. Place the leaves together to form a mat and stand the fish in the middle. Spread the coconut paste thickly over each side and wrap in the leaves, then in aluminum foil. Cook the fish slowly in the barbecue, turning several times, until done (approximately 45 minutes).

WHOLE FISH IN SPICY COCONUT BAKED IN BANANA LEAVES

RUJAK FRUIT AND VEGETABLE SALAD

Rujak Fruit and Vegetable Salad

▲▲▲▲▲▲

1 nashi (Japanese pear) or ¼ bangkuang
(yam bean) or
1 cake (3½ oz / 100 g) compressed (hard)
beancurd (tofu)
2-3 tablespoons vegetable oil
1 unripe mango or 8 oz (250 g) unripe papaya
(pawpaw)
1 carambola (star fruit)
1 small cucumber
1 salad onion
1 firm banana
2 thick slices pineapple or jackfruit
5 oz (150 g) fresh mung bean spouts
lettuce leaves

Dressing:
2 teaspoons concentrated tamarind
⅓ cup (3 fl oz / 100 ml) boiling water
½ teaspoon blachan (compressed shrimp paste)
1-2 fresh red chilies, seeded and minced
2 tablespoons sweet soy sauce
sugar to taste

First prepare the dressing by infusing tamarind in boiling water. Strain into a small mixing bowl or screwtop jar. Wrap the shrimp paste in a small square of aluminum foil and cook for 2-3 minutes in a hot pan, unwrap and crumble before adding to the tamarind with the other sauce ingredients. Whisk or shake to combine and set aside to cool.

Peel the yam bean and slice it thinly. Blanch in boiling, salted water for 2-3 minutes and drain. If using the pear, peel, slice into segments and soak in lightly salted cold water. Thinly slice the beancurd cake and fry in the oil until lightly browned, remove with a slotted spoon. Place on absorbent paper to drain and cool.

Peel and slice the mango or papaya. Slice the carambola, cucumber and cut the onion into wedges. Slice the banana thickly. Peel the pineapple or jackfruit and cut it into wedges. Blanch the bean sprouts briefly, then cover with cold water to cool and firm them. Drain well.

Combine the salad ingredients in a mixing bowl with the dressing. Spread lettuce on a serving platter and mound the salad in the middle. Serve lightly chilled.

RIJSTAFFEL ACCOMPANIMENTS

Rijstaffel Accompaniments

▲▲▲▲▲▲

Rijstaffel accompaniments include crisply fried shrimp flakes and spicy little side dishes known as sambals. These can be placed on the table at the beginning of the meal, or served with the main course. You might like to also offer sliced, hard-boiled eggs, sliced cucumber, wedges of pineapple or jackfruit segments and roasted peanuts.

Shrimp Crisps

To cook shrimp crisps, heat deep-frying oil and very briefly fry the crisps no more than three or four at a time, until they expand and float to the surface. Retrieve from the oil on a skimmer and drain on absorbent paper before serving.

Tomato Sambal

Cut 3 small, well-ripened tomatoes into halves and 3 small salad onions into thin slices. Combine 1 tablespoon soy sauce with 1 teaspoon sambal ulek and sugar to taste. Add a little vegetable oil and 1 tablespoon finely chopped mint, basil or coriander. Pour dressing over the tomatoes and stir lightly, chill briefly before serving.

Coconut Chili Sambal

Combine 1 teaspoon blachan (compressed shrimp paste) with 6 tablespoons desiccated or finely shredded coconut and 1¼ teaspoons chili flakes in a food processor. Grind to a powder and add salt and sugar to taste. Transfer to a screwtop jar and store in a cool place until needed. This sambal will keep for several weeks.

Turmeric Rice

▲▲▲▲▲▲

2 ¾ cups (20 oz / 625 g) long-grain white rice
⅓ cup (30 g) shredded (desiccated) coconut
1 cup (8 fl oz / 250 ml) thick coconut milk
(cream)
3 cups (24 fl oz / 750 ml) light chicken stock
1½ teaspoons ground turmeric
salt
2 Kaffir lime leaves (optional)

In a saucepan with a heavy base combine the rice and coconut with salt and turmeric. Add coconut milk and stock and bring briskly to the boil. Cook uncovered for 1 minute, then stir, cover the pan tightly and reduce heat to the minimum setting.

Cook undisturbed for 15 minutes. Lift the lid, stir the contents and replace the lid. Let the rice sit for 10-15 minutes before using.

Lychee Mousse

▲▲▲▲▲▲

2 x 20 oz (560 g) cans lychees in syrup
1½ tablespoons plain gelatine
1 cup (8 fl oz / 250 ml) light sour cream
1½ tablespoons crystallized ginger, finely diced
2-3 cups tropical fruit to garnish, diced
1 cup (8 fl oz / 250 ml) cream
1 tablespoon Cointreau (optional)

Drain the lychees, reserving the liquid, and pour them into a food processor. Blend to a smooth puree. Add all but ½ cup of their liquid and blend again briefly.

Heat the reserved liquid in a small saucepan, add the gelatine and stir to dissolve. Pour over the lychees and add the sour cream and ginger. Blend without overbeating.

Pour the mixture into a wet tin and refrigerate until set. Turn out onto a dessert plate and fill with the fruit. Whip the cream, add Cointreau and serve separately.

LYCHEE MOUSSE

A NIGHT IN BANGKOK

Serves 6-8

Marinated Seafood Salad with Herbed Oysters on the Half Shell

Sliced Fish with a Ginger Sauce

Green Duck Curry

Shredded Papaya (Pawpaw) Salad

Thai Fried Rice with Crabmeat

Coconut Bananas on Caramel Sauce

This menu combines a group of delightful Thai dishes which lend themselves to elegant presentation. The first course is made up of two classic dishes which should be served together. The marinated seafood in its profusion of herbs has a salty-citrus dressing smoothed with coconut milk, a typical taste combination. The oysters, served on the half shell, exemplify another Thai taste partnership of lemon grass, chili and coriander.

As the curry has a rich and assertive sauce, I have balanced it with the milder ginger taste of the fish. The salad, with its pleasant lemon tang, will help the palate assimilate the myriad seasonings. You may choose to simplify the menu by cooking plain Jasmine rice.

A dessert of distinction was needed to complete this meal. The fried bananas bring crispness, countered by the delicious nuttiness of the coconut caramel.

When my guests are seated I bring out a well-chilled muscadet. With the green duck curry serve a chilled sparkling red burgundy or a Gewertztraminer – the sweetness works well with the intense curry.

Marinated Seafood Salad with Herbed Oysters on the Half Shell

▲▲▲▲▲▲

Marinated Seafood Salad:

1½ lb (750 g) mixed seafood (white fish such as cod, fresh tuna, scallops, peeled small shrimp, small squid)
¼ cup (2 fl oz / 60 ml) lime juice
3 tablespoons Thai fish sauce
1 cup (8 fl oz / 250 ml) thin coconut milk
⅓ teaspoon cracked black pepper
3 scallions (spring onions), trimmed
2 medium tomatoes, skinned and seeded
8 small lettuce leaves
8 sprigs fresh coriander
8 sprigs fresh mint
8 sprigs fresh basil
very finely shredded red and green chili pepper, soaked in ice-water to curl (optional)

Herbed Oysters on the Half Shell:

24 fresh oysters in the half shell
1 tablespoon fresh ginger, grated
1 tablespoon lemon grass, very finely minced
1 tablespoon fresh coriander, very finely chopped
2 teaspoons fresh red chili, very finely minced
cracked black pepper
lime wedges

Cut the seafood into paper-thin slices crosswise and place in a wide dish. Combine the lime juice, fish sauce, coconut milk and pepper and pour over the fish. Cover with clingwrap and refrigerate for 5-6 hours.

Very thinly slice the scallions and finely dice the tomato. Place a lettuce leaf on each plate, fill with the fish and garnish with the herbs. Arrange shredded chili on top, if used.

Arrange 3 oysters on each plate. Place the ginger in a small piece of clean cloth and squeeze a few drops of ginger juice on each oyster. Arrange a few pieces of the lemon grass, coriander and chili between the oyster and shell and season with black pepper. Place a lime wedge on each plate and serve at once.

MARINATED SEAFOOD SALAD WITH HERBED OYSTERS ON THE HALF SHELL

SLICED FISH WITH A GINGER SAUCE

Sliced Fish with a Ginger Sauce

▲▲▲▲▲▲

Ginger Sauce:

5 dried black mushrooms, soaked
2 tablespoons vegetable oil
1 medium onion, finely sliced
2 scallions (spring onions), trimmed and shredded
1-2 fresh red chili peppers, seeded and shredded
2 inch (5 cm) piece fresh, young ginger, finely shredded
⅓ cup (3 ¼ oz / 85 ml) distilled white vinegar
½ cup (3 ¾ oz / 110 g) fine white sugar
salt and cracked black pepper
¾ cup (6 fl oz / 180 ml) fish stock or water
1 tablespoon cornstarch (cornflour)

Fish:

1½ lb (750 g) thick white fish fillets, skinned
1 tablespoon fresh ginger, grated
salt and white pepper
cornstarch (cornflour)
oil for deep-frying

To make the sauce, drain the mushrooms squeezing out excess water, cut off the tough stems and shred the caps finely. Heat oil in a medium-sized saucepan and sauté onion until softened but not brown. Add the remaining ingredients except cornstarch and bring to the boil. Simmer for 5 minutes.

Stir cornstarch into 2 tablespoons cold water, pour into sauce and stir until it thickens and becomes translucent. Remove from the heat and keep warm.

Heat oil for deep-frying in a large pan or wok. Cut fish across the fillets into thick fingers. Place ginger in a piece of clean cloth and squeeze juice over the fish. Season with salt and pepper and coat with cornstarch.

Fry the fish for about 5 minutes until golden, then drain well. Arrange on a platter and pour on the hot sauce. Garnish with carrot flowers and sprigs of parsley or fresh coriander and serve.

To make carrot flowers, peel a long thin carrot. Using the point of a narrow-bladed, very sharp knife, push it at a sharp diagonal angle downward into the carrot 1 inch (2.5 cm) from the tip. Make four identical cuts around the tip of the carrot and pull off the tip which now resembles a little flower. Continue in this way up the stem of the carrot.

GREEN DUCK CURRY

Green Duck Curry

▲▲▲▲▲▲

Green Thai curry paste (see page 28)
2 x 14 fl oz (440 ml) cans thick coconut
milk (cream)
1 large duck, approx 4 lb (2 kg)
1 large onion, sliced finely
2 tablespoons vegetable oil
8 dried Kaffir lime leaves, soaked
1½ teaspoons salt
14 fl oz (440 ml) can thin coconut milk
½ cup loosely packed fresh basil leaves
lime juice and fish sauce to taste

Prepare the curry paste (see page 28). Pour 1 can thick coconut milk into a saucepan and bring almost to the boil. Cook, slowly stirring, until it is well reduced and the oil has separated. Add the curry paste and simmer for 5 minutes.

Cut the duck into 2 inch (5 cm) pieces. Add to the curry and cook over low heat until the curry paste clings to the duck pieces (about 10 minutes).

In another pan sauté the onion until golden, add the lime leaves, salt, remaining thick coconut milk and the thin coconut milk and bring just to the boil. Reduce heat and simmer for 10 minutes.

Pour over the duck and place in a moderate oven, or simmer on top of the stove, for about 45 minutes, until the duck is tender. Add basil leaves, and season to taste with lime juice and fish sauce.

Shredded Papaya (Pawpaw) Salad
(Som Tam)

▲▲▲▲▲▲

1 large unripe papaya (pawpaw)
¼ cup (1 oz / 25 g) dried shrimp, soaked in boiling water
½-1 tablespoon chili flakes
4-5 cloves garlic, very finely chopped
lime juice and Thai fish sauce to taste
sugar to taste

Peel the papaya, cut in halves and scrape out the unformed white seeds. Coarsely grate the papaya into a salad bowl.

Drain the shrimp, place in a mortar with chili flakes and garlic and grind to a paste. Add lime juice, fish sauce and sugar to your taste (it should be strong, hot and quite tart). Fold through the papaya and chill lightly before serving.

SHREDDED PAPAYA (PAWPAW) SALAD

THAI FRIED RICE WITH CRABMEAT

Thai Fried Rice with Crabmeat

▲▲▲▲▲▲

3 cups (1¼ lb / 675 g) long-grain Jasmine rice
4 cups (32 fl oz / 1 l) water
1 teaspoon salt
1 large onion
2 tablespoons vegetable oil
1-2 cloves garlic, chopped very finely
6 oz (180 g) fresh bean sprouts
7 oz (210 g) cooked crabmeat
¾ teaspoon white pepper
1½ tablespoons Thai fish sauce
2 scallion (spring onion) tops, shredded finely
1 fresh red chili pepper, seeded and shredded finely
2 tablespoons roasted peanuts, finely chopped

Place the rice in a heavy saucepan with water and salt. Bring quickly to a brisk boil, then cover tightly. Reduce heat to the lowest temperature setting and cook for about 15 minutes undisturbed.

Cut top and base from onion and slice vertically into narrow strips. Sauté in the oil until softened but not deeply browned, add garlic and sauté briefly. Add bean sprouts and crabmeat and cook for 1-2 minutes.

Stir into the rice, adding the pepper and fish sauce. Serve garnished with scallion tops, chili and peanuts.

Coconut Bananas on Caramel Sauce

▲▲▲▲▲▲

8 small firm bananas
¾ cup (3½ oz / 110 g) all-purpose (plain) flour
3 eggs, lightly beaten
4 oz (120 g) shredded coconut
⅓ cup (1½ oz / 45 g) fine, dry breadcrumbs
oil for deep frying

Caramel Sauce:
¾ cup (3½ oz / 110 g) brown sugar
¾ cup (6 oz / 180 g) white sugar
¾ cup (6 fl oz / 180 ml) water
14 fl oz (440 ml) can thick coconut milk (cream)
1½ tablespoons cornstarch (cornflour)

Cut the bananas in halves, then slice each half lengthwise in two. Place in a plastic bag with the flour and shake to coat evenly. Remove and shake off excess flour, dip into beaten egg. Combine coconut and crumbs. Coat the bananas, then chill for 1 hour.

In a saucepan suited to cooking sugar, dissolve the sugars in the water and cook at a very gentle boil until golden brown. Remove from the heat and carefully stir in the coconut milk. Return to the heat and cook until a smooth sauce forms.

Blend cornstarch with a little water, stir into the sauce and cook, stirring continuously until thickened. Remove from the heat and keep warm until required.

Heat the oil to moderately hot in a large pan or wok. Deep-fry the bananas in several batches until the surface is golden. Drain well. Spread the sauce over dessert plates and arrange several pieces of banana on each. Serve at once.

COCONUT BANANAS ON CARAMEL SAUCE

THE SPICES OF SICHUAN

Serves 8-10

Pickled Cucumbers with Crispy Peanuts

Hot and Sour Soup

Chicken 'Gung Pao'

Dry-fried Beef with Sesame and Orange Peel

Stuffed Beancurd in Vegetable Casserole

Poached Ginger Pears

I have a long-standing love affair with the food of Sichuan, China's central-western province. The adventurous palate is seduced by pungent bean pastes and garlic, titillated by chilies and ginger, teased by intense sweet-hot-tangy tastes.

This is the birthplace of many of China's best cooks, where formal banquets begin with an array of cold dishes to nibble with potent rice wine, and anything up to sixty dishes to follow.

We begin this meal with crisp, chili hot cucumber slices to accustom the palate to the complex and intense character of the classic hot and sour soup. The trio of main dishes can all be brought to the table together, with plenty of white rice to nullify the bite of the chilies. Together they offer a multitude of tastes and textures. The chicken dish is fresh and attractive; the beef, crisp and slightly chewy with an interesting underlying flavor of orange. The beancurd casserole introduces typical Chinese vegetables in a smooth-crisp combination.

I do not think a grape wine can do justice to the classic Sichuan Hot and Sour Soup. Serve rice wine or sake, gently warmed, neat cognac, whiskey or perhaps an excellent dry sherry to begin. These main dishes are somewhat more restrained than is usual for Sichuan food (pep them up if you like with extra chili) so offer a slightly fruity white wine. I suggest a finale of a medium to dry champagne with the light dessert.

Pickled Cucumbers with Crispy Peanuts

▲▲▲▲▲▲

6 small continental acid-free cucumbers
1 fresh red chili pepper
1½ teaspoons salt
⅓ cup (3½ fl oz / 85 ml) distilled white vinegar
¼ cup (2 oz / 60 g) white sugar
¼ - ½ teaspoon chili oil
2 teaspoons sesame oil
1 cup (7 oz / 210 g) peanuts, shelled
oil for deep frying

Wash and dry the cucumber. Cut in half lengthwise, and then halve again crosswise. Place a piece of cucumber on a board, skin side upward. Use a sharp knife to fan by cutting into very thin slices, but not quite cutting through to the board. This way the pickling liquid can penetrate, but the cucumber will remain as a whole piece. Place the prepared cucumber in a glass or stainless steel dish.

Cut the pepper in half and scrape out the seeds, cut it crosswise into thin slices. Scatter evenly over the cucumber and sprinkle with salt.

Heat the vinegar and sugar until very hot but not boiling, add chili and sesame oil. Pour over the cucumber and leave to cool.

Deep-fry the peanuts in oil until crisp and golden, then drain on absorbent paper. Drain the cucumber, arrange on two or three plates with the peanuts and serve.

PICKLED CUCUMBERS WITH CRISPY PEANUTS

HOT AND SOUR SOUP

Hot and Sour Soup

▲▲▲▲▲▲

3 oz (90 g) lean pork
3 oz (90 g) pork or calf liver
3 oz (90 g) chicken breast
8 dried black mushrooms, soaked
¾ oz (20 g) black wood ear fungus, soaked
¾ oz (20 g) tiger lily buds (golden needles), soaked
2 oz (60 g) canned bamboo shoots
8 cups (64 fl oz / 2 l) chicken stock or water
1¼ inch (3 cm) piece fresh ginger, shredded finely
1 clove garlic, chopped finely
1 tablespoon dark soy sauce
1 teaspoon chili oil
2 tablespoons Chinese black vinegar
½ teaspoon ground Sichuan peppercorns
3 eggs, lightly beaten and strained
2 cakes soft beancurd

2 tablespoons cornstarch (cornflour)
5 scallions (spring onions), chopped
salt
light soy sauce
additional chili oil and Chinese black vinegar

Cut all of the meat and vegetables into very fine shreds.

In a large soup pot, bring the stock or water to the boil, add ginger, garlic and soy sauce and simmer for 3-4 minutes. Add the shredded ingredients, vinegar, sugar, chili oil and pepper. Reduce heat and simmer for 10 minutes.

Pour the beaten eggs into the hot soup in a thin stream so that it sets immediately into strands. Cut beancurd into small cubes and add to the soup. Mix cornstarch with cold water and pour into soup, adding the scallions. Simmer briefly, stirring throughout. Season with salt or soy sauce, or both, and adjust the amount of chili oil and black vinegar to taste. This dish is typically quite hot and tart.

CHICKEN 'GUNG PAO'

Chicken 'Gung Pao'

▲▲▲▲▲▲

1 lb (500 g) boneless chicken breast
2-3 cloves garlic, finely chopped
¾ inch (2 cm) piece fresh ginger, finely shredded
2 tablespoons yellow rice wine
2 tablespoons light soy sauce
1 teaspoon sugar
¾ cup (6 fl oz / 180 ml) vegetable oil
2 teaspoons sesame oil
3 fresh red chili peppers, seeded and sliced
½ cup (3½ oz / 100 g) shelled raw peanuts
3 scallions (spring onions), chopped
¾ cup (6 fl oz / 180 ml) chicken stock

2 teaspoons cornstarch (cornflour)
Chinese black vinegar
finely ground Sichuan peppercorns

Cut the chicken into ¾ inch (2 cm) cubes and place in a dish with the garlic, ginger, wine, soy sauce and sugar. Mix well and marinate for 20 minutes.

Heat the oils in a wok. Stir-fry the chili and peanuts for 2 minutes. Add the chicken and stir-fry for 2-3 minutes. Add the scallions and stock mixed with cornstarch and cook, stirring, over high heat until the sauce thickens.

Add vinegar and pepper, plus a little salt if needed, to taste. Stir in and serve over rice.

Dry-fried Beef with Sesame and Orange Peel

▲▲▲▲▲▲

14 oz (410 g) rump or fillet (tenderloin) steak
1 tablespoon dark soy sauce
1 tablespoon yellow rice wine
1½ teaspoons fresh ginger, finely grated
4 x ¾ inch (2 cm) squares dried orange peel
2 teaspoons cornstarch (cornflour)
3 dried red chilies, roughly chopped
2 cups (16 fl oz / 500 ml) vegetable oil
2 teaspoons sesame oil
3 scallions (spring onions), sliced
1 tablespoon light soy sauce

Cut the steak across the grain into paper-thin slices and then into strips about 1 x 2 inches (2.5 cm x 5 cm). Place in a dish and pour on the soy sauce and wine, adding ginger, orange peel and cornstarch and mixing well. Set aside to marinate for 45 minutes.

Heat the oil and fry chilies until crisp. Add beef and fry for 7-8 minutes until very well-cooked. Remove on a slotted spoon and pour off the oil. Return beef and chilies to the pan, add sesame oil, scallions and soy sauce and stir-fry for 2 minutes. Serve with white rice.

DRY-FRIED BEEF WITH SESAME AND ORANGE PEEL

STUFFED BEANCURD IN VEGETABLE CASSEROLE

Stuffed Beancurd in Vegetable Casserole

▲▲▲▲▲▲

1 cake (4 x 7 inches / 10 x 18 cm) soft fresh beancurd
2 oz (60 g) very finely minced (ground) pork
2 teaspoons finely minced scallion (spring onion)
½ teaspoon finely minced fresh ginger
cornstarch (cornflour)
frying oil
12-18 small dried mushrooms, soaked
1 oz (30 g) black wood ear fungus, soaked
3 cups (24 fl oz / 750 ml) chicken stock or water
3 oz (90 g) canned bamboo shoots, thickly sliced
1 medium carrot, thickly sliced
3 large scallions (spring onions), sliced
3 oz (90 g) canned straw mushrooms, halved
12 cauliflower flowerets
1 large tomato, cut into wedges
6 baby bok choy vegetables, halved lengthwise
10 thin slices fresh ginger
2 tablespoons oyster sauce
salt and / or light soy sauce
2 teaspoons Chinese red vinegar (optional)

Cut the beancurd into manageable cubes and use a teaspoon to remove a portion from the middle of each. Combine the pork, minced scallion and ginger and mix to a smooth paste. Dust the beancurd with cornstarch, press the filling into the cavity and dust again.

Heat 1 inch (3 cm) oil in a small pan and fry the stuffed beancurd until the filling is cooked, about 3 minutes, turning once; remove and set aside.

Drain mushrooms and remove stems. Drain black fungus and chop roughly. Boil the stock or water in an ovenproof casserole dish or heavy saucepan. Add ginger, mushrooms and fungus and simmer for 3 minutes. Add the vegetables and simmer for about 15 minutes or until tender and the stock is well seasoned.

Season with the oyster sauce and salt or soy sauce. Stir 2 tablespoons cornstarch into a half cup of water and stir into the sauce to thicken. Add the beancurd and heat through gently. Stir in vinegar, if used, just before serving.

Poached Ginger Pears

▲▲▲▲▲▲

8 nashi (Japanese pears) or other pears
2 tablespoons glacé fruit, finely diced
1 tablespoon glacé ginger, diced
8 red glacé cherries
4 oz (125 g) Chinese rock sugar, crushed
6 slices fresh ginger

Peel and core the pears and stand in a heat-proof serving dish. Combine the glacé fruit and ginger and fill the cavities of the pears. Spread the rock sugar evenly in the dish, add the sliced ginger.

Place in a steamer, cover and cook over gently simmering water for about 20 minutes until the pears are tender.

Spoon some of the accumulated syrup over the pears to serve.

POACHED GINGER PEARS

DELICACIES FROM JAPAN

Serves 6

Scallop Nori Rolls

Tuna Sashimi

Seared Garlic Beef with Lime Sauce

Seaweed, Cucumber and Crabmeat Salad

Fried Beancurd in Sauce

Miso-broiled Chicken Wings with Rice

Sliced Fruit over Ice

Japanese meals are composed of a number of small dishes, chosen to complement each other, and to present a variety of cooking styles and ingredients. Each course is quite small, little more than a few bites, and cooking time is short and the sauces uncomplicated.

This meal begins with crisply coated *nori* rolls to introduce the distinct tastes that are exclusively Japanese. The *sashimi* follows so that the palate can fully appreciate the delicate taste and smooth texture of the raw fish. The remaining courses can be brought out together or in succession, depending on your kitchen and cooking arrangements. Each dish has distinct texture and taste highlights. The beancurd a contrast of creamy bland and salty, the beef marrying lime and garlic, and the chicken wings crisp on the surface, succulent within.

Serve white rice in covered bowls on the side, and you might also like to offer a clear soup. Buy instant soups from your Japanese food stockist and add a few fresh ingredients such as a slice of mushroom, a sliver of lemon rind or a single fresh shrimp in its shell.

Japanese food can leave the palate with a sensation of dryness, so iced fruit is an excellent, and typical, way to end the meal. Slice crisp red apples and nashi (Japanese pears), melons or kiwi fruit and serve them over ice. Alternatively, bathe melon balls in Midori and serve on finely shaved ice.

Scallop Nori Rolls

▲▲▲▲▲▲

4-5 large sheets nori (compressed seaweed)
40 pieces (1 lb / 500 g) sea scallops
1 tablespoon mirin (Japanese sherry)
1 tablespoon light soy sauce (tamari)
2 scallions (spring onions), chopped very finely
2 teaspoons grated fresh ginger
1½ cups (8 oz / 185 g) all-purpose (plain) flour

2 eggs, lightly beaten
1¼-½ cups (10-12 fl oz / 310-375 ml) iced water
deep-frying oil

Hold the nori sheets over a flame for a few seconds to crisp, cut each in half and set aside. Marinate the scallops in the mirin, soy sauce, scallions and ginger for 15 minutes.

Drain the scallops and place 5 pieces in the middle of each sheet of nori. Roll into a cylinder. Moisten the edge and the ends to stick down.

Heat oil for deep frying. Sift flour into a mixing bowl and add the eggs and enough iced water to make a light batter. Mix it sparingly, so there are still little pockets of unmixed flour.

Coat the nori rolls with the batter and slide into the oil. Fry until the surface is crisp and golden, lift out on a slotted spoon to drain. Cut each roll in half and serve at once.

Tuna Sashimi

▲▲▲▲▲▲

This will be a small course, just a few cubes per person. You may serve plain light (tamari) soy sauce pepped up with wasabi (Japanese horseradish) as the dip, or make up this sauce the night before.

Dipping Sauce:
1 tablespoon sake
3 tablespoons mirin (Japanese sherry)
4 inch (10 cm) square kombu kelp, scored with a sharp knife
1 tablespoon sugar
¼ cup (2 fl oz / 60 ml) light soy sauce
¾ cup (8 fl oz / 180 ml) dark soy sauce
2 tablespoons dried bonito flakes

Boil sake and mirin in a small saucepan until reduced by half. Add rinsed and dried kombu kelp and sugar, stir to dissolve and let stand until cool. Add soy sauces and bonito flakes and cover. Stand overnight, strain to use.

12 oz (375 g) fresh tuna (preferably taken from the belly section which has a richer taste)
2 small lemons
8 small sprigs of greenery to garnish
wasabi (Japanese horseradish)

Using a sharp knife with a thin blade, slice the fish into thin strips or into ½ inch (1.25 cm) cubes. Arrange them artistically on small plates. Slice the lemon and garnish the plates with lemon slices and sprigs of greenery. Mix wasabi powder with cold water or sake to make a thick paste. Place a little mound of the wasabi on each plate.

Serve the dipping sauce in small dishes. A smear of the wasabi is stirred into the sauce before you begin to eat.

TUNA SASHIMI

Seared Garlic Beef with Lime Sauce

▲▲▲▲▲▲

10 oz (300 g) piece eye fillet (tenderloin) steak
4 cloves garlic, chopped very finely
1 teaspoon salt
2 tablespoons vegetable oil

Lime Sauce:
1 tablespoon mirin (Japanese sherry)
¼ cup (2 fl oz / 60 ml) fresh lime juice
1 tablespoon sugar
3 tablespoons light soy sauce

Trim the steak to remove any filaments, fat or surface clear tissue. Mash the garlic with salt and spread evenly over the meat, wrap up firmly in clingwrap and chill thoroughly.

Heat the mirin in a small saucepan until it boils, then remove from heat. Add remaining sauce ingredients and set aside to cool.

Heat a hotplate and rub the surface with a piece of paper towel dipped in oil. When the hotplate is very hot, sear the surface of the meat. When done, the meat will be cooked to a depth of about ⅓ inch (1 cm).

Slice the beef very thinly and arrange on a platter. Pour the sauce into a small dip dish and set in the middle of the meat. Serve at once.

SEAWEED, CUCUMBER AND CRABMEAT SALAD

Seaweed, Cucumber and Crabmeat Salad

▲▲▲▲▲▲

½ oz (15 g) dried wakame or hijiki seaweed, soaked in warm water
2 small continental-style cucumbers
salt
6 oz (180 g) cooked crabmeat
¼ cup (2 fl oz / 60 ml) Japanese rice vinegar
3 tablespoons light soy sauce
2½ teaspoons sugar

Drain the seaweed and cover with fresh cold water. Cut the cucumbers in half lengthwise and slice thinly. If you like, scrape out the seeds with a teaspoon or melon baller. Sprinkle with salt and set aside. Break up the crabmeat, but do not shred too finely.

Drain the seaweed, dry by shaking in a cloth, then slice any larger pieces. Combine the ingredients together on individual salad plates.

Shake the vinegar, soy and sugar in a screwtop jar, pour over the salad and let stand for 15 minutes before serving.

SEARED GARLIC BEEF WITH LIME SAUCE

Fried Beancurd in Sauce

▲▲▲▲▲▲

2-3 cakes soft fresh beancurd
¾ cup (2 oz / 60 g) arrowroot or tapioca starch
oil for deep-frying
3 scallions (spring onions), chopped very finely
3 inch (8 cm) piece daikon (giant white radish),
very finely grated
⅓ cup (3 fl oz / 85 ml) mirin (Japanese sherry)
2½ tablespoons light soy sauce
1½ cups (12 fl oz / 375 ml) Japanese dashi stock
1 teaspoon sugar

Take a piece of beancurd in the hand and use a thin bladed sharp knife to carefully cut it on the palm of the hand into ¼ inch (3 cm) cubes. Coat with the flour and set aside for 10 minutes.

Heat oil and carefully fry the beancurd until the surface is slightly crisped and golden, transfer to a serving dish or small Japanese style dishes, using a slotted spoon to drain them well.

Scatter scallions and grated daikon over each piece. In a small saucepan heat the mirin and simmer for 1 minute, add the soy, stock and sugar and simmer for 2 minutes. Pour over the beancurd and serve at once.

MISO-BROILED CHICKEN WINGS

Miso-broiled Chicken Wings

▲▲▲▲▲▲

16-20 chicken wings (tip and middle joints only)
white pepper
1 cup (8 oz / 250 g) white miso paste
2 tablespoons sugar
2 tablespoons vegetable oil

Rinse, drain and dry the wings. Sprinkle with pepper. In a small dish combine the miso with sugar, 1 tablespoon of the oil and enough water to make a thick paste, about ½ cup. Spread over the chicken wings and set aside for 1 hour to firm up.

Broil (grill) the wings slowly, preferably over glowing charcoal, until the surface is well crisped and the meat cooked through.

Fill individual-serving lacquer boxes, bowls or plates with white rice and place two wings on each dish.

Sliced Fruit over Ice

▲▲▲▲▲▲

Arrange finely sliced fruit of your own preference over a flat dish of crushed ice, for a typical Asian dessert.

FRIED BEANCURD IN SAUCE

EASTERN ALFRESCO

Serves 12-20

Pork Satay with Peanut Sauce

Vegetable Samoosas

Noodles in Spicy Coconut Curry with Shrimp

Beef Rendang

Rice with Green Peas and Onion

Guava Mousse with Fruit Salad

Cooking for a large dinner party is easy if you plan ahead. To start the meal I have chosen two special Asian dishes, followed by my Indonesian Rendang, which should be cooked a day or two in advance to achieve its true potential. In this menu I team it with *laksa*.

A spicy meal demands piquant chutneys and pickles. Purchase several different styles of hot and sweet pickles and Indian-style chutneys. Have baskets of crisp *krupuk* (fried shrimp flakes) or *poppadams* on the table. Easy-to-make curry accompaniments include diced tomato and cucumber sprinkled with chopped mint, halved hard-boiled eggs dusted with cayenne pepper or paprika, salads of cubed pineapple sprinkled with sugar, coriander leaves and chili flakes, cooked sliced carrot sprinkled with aniseed, cucumber sticks marinated in vinegar with a touch of sugar and chili, and sliced banana sprinkled with lime juice and covered with toasted shredded coconut. Serve garnished with fresh herbs, onion rings and lime wedges.

Begin with cocktails. Perhaps white rum with tropical fruit juices and a splash of coconut milk. Sauvignon Blanc Semillon white wine or a fairly substantial rosé or beaujolais would be a good accompaniment to the main course.

Pork Satay with Peanut Sauce

▲▲▲▲▲▲

4 quantities spicy peanut sauce (see below)
4 lb (2 kg) lean pork
4 cloves garlic, peeled
2 large onions, peeled
1 fresh red chili, seeded
1 lemon grass stalk, trimmed
1 teaspoon blachan (compressed shrimp paste)
1½ tablespoons ground coriander
1½ teaspoons ground turmeric
2 teaspoons laos (galangal) powder
1½ teaspoons salt
1 teaspoon cracked black pepper
2 teaspoons tamarind concentrate
2 teaspoons sugar
2 cups (16 fl oz / 500 ml) coconut milk
vegetable oil
40 thin bamboo skewers, soaked in water

Prepare the sauce and set aside. Cut the pork into ¾ inch (2 cm) cubes or into long narrow strips. Thread three cubes or weave one strip of pork onto each skewer. Arrange them on a wide flat tray.

Grind the garlic, onions, chili, lemon grass and blachan in a food processor until smooth. Add the spices, seasonings, tamarind, sugar and coconut milk and blend together. Add 2 tablespoons vegetable oil and blend again.

Pour the mixture evenly over the satay and cover. Refrigerate for 4-12 hours, turning the meat every hour.

When ready to cook, heat charcoal or gas barbecue. Brush the satay with vegetable oil and broil (grill) until the surface is flecked with deep-brown and the meat cooked but still tender and moist inside.

Spread the sauce onto flat dishes and serve with the hot satay and cubed cucumber.

Spicy Peanut Sauce

▲▲▲▲▲▲

Toast one tablespoon of coriander seeds in the oven or a dry frying pan. Grind finely. Then toast ½ teaspoon of shrimp paste for 1 or 2 minutes. Very finely mince 2 gloves of garlic and 1 small onion and saute in 3 tablespoons of vegetable oil until well-cooked. Add the seeds and paste plus half a chopped lemon-grass stalk, 1 to 2 teaspoons of chili sauce, 5 oz (150 gms) crunchy peanut butter and ¾ cup (6 fl oz / 180 ml) of thick coconut milk. Simmer for 2 to 3 minutes. Season with salt, pepper and lime juice.

PORK SATAY WITH PEANUT SAUCE

VEGETABLE SAMOOSAS

Vegetable Samoosas

▲▲▲▲▲▲

1 pack frozen large egg roll (spring roll)
wrappers
¾ lb (375 g) potatoes (or use finely minced
beef or lamb)
½ inch (1.5 cm) piece fresh ginger, chopped finely
3 cloves garlic, chopped finely
3 tablespoons vegetable oil
½ lb (250 g) shelled fresh or frozen peas
1-2 fresh green chilies, seeded and minced
½ teaspoon ground turmeric
1 tablespoon ground coriander
¾ teaspoons ground cumin
1 teaspoon garam masala
1 tablespoon chopped fresh coriander
1 tablespoon lemon juice
oil for deep-frying

Thaw the egg roll wrappers under a cloth to prevent drying out.

Peel and finely dice the potatoes and sauté with the ginger and garlic in half the oil for 2-3 minutes. Add ½ cup water, cover and cook gently until they are very tender.

Boil peas in lightly salted water until just tender. Drain and mix with potatoes. Heat the remaining oil in a small pan and fry the spices for 1 minute until very aromatic. Pour this over the vegetables and leave to cool. Stir in the coriander and lemon juice.

To make the samoosas, cut the egg roll wrappers into 1¾ inch (4 cm) strips. Place a portion of filling at the end and fold an edge diagonally over. Continue to fold around the filling to make triangular pastries. Seal the loose edge with water. The samoosas can be prepared in advance and refrigerated until needed.

Sprinkle cornstarch lightly over a tray, arrange samoosas side-by-side and sprinkle on more cornstarch, cover with plastic wrap and arrange another layer on top. Seal completely. To fry frozen samoosas, partially thaw them and then fry in moderately hot oil allowing time to heat all the way through.

To fry fresh samoosas, heat oil to very hot, then reduce the heat slightly. Fry them in batches of 6 to 8, for about 1½ minutes until golden. Drain well and serve hot. Bottled tamarind sauce is an ideal accompaniment.

Noodles in Spicy Coconut Curry with Shrimp

▲▲▲▲▲▲

4 large onions, sliced very finely
4 tablespoons vegetable oil
3 tablespoons coriander seeds
3 lemon grass stalks, trimmed and chopped
3 x 14 fl oz (440 ml) cans coconut milk
2 teaspoons cumin seeds
½ teaspoon caraway seeds
½ teaspoon black peppercorns
1½ teaspoons blachan (compressed shrimp paste)
8 cloves garlic, peeled
1½ inch (4 cm) piece fresh ginger, peeled

2 oz (60 g) kemiri (candlenuts) or macadamia nuts, ground finely
¾ inch (2 cm) piece fresh turmeric or 1⅓ teaspoons ground turmeric
5 dried Kaffir lime leaves, soaked
2-3 dried red chilies, soaked
1½ lb (750 g) small fresh shrimp, shelled
1 lb (500 g) rice vermicelli, soaked
3 tablespoons chopped fresh coriander
3 tablespoons crisp-fried onions

Sauté the onions in 3 tablespoons oil until well softened, then remove half and set aside. Continue to cook the remaining half of the onions until they are a very deep brown.

Toast the coriander seeds in the oven or a dry pan until aromatic and beginning to pop. Grind finely. In one saucepan place the sautéed onions, one-third of the coriander and 1 tablespoon chopped lemon grass. Add 1 can of the coconut milk and bring almost to the boil. Reduce the heat and simmer for 20 minutes, stirring occasionally. Season and remove from the heat.

Toast the cumin, caraway seeds and peppercorns until aromatic and then grind them finely. In another pan, heat the remaining oil and fry the shrimp paste until pungent. Add the garlic, ginger, nuts and remaining lemon grass and fry for 2 minutes, add turmeric and fry briefly. Transfer to a spice grinder or mortar and grind to a paste. Return to the saucepan and add the lime leaves, chilies and remaining coconut milk. Add 2 cups water. Bring to the boil, reduce heat and simmer for 30 minutes, stirring occasionally. Season to taste with salt, pepper and fish sauce.

Add shrimp to the dark onion sauce and simmer until tender, about 6 minutes. Add drained vermicelli to the other sauce and simmer for the same time.

Place the vermicelli into a large deep dish and pour the shrimp sauce over it. Garnish with the coriander and crisp-fried onion.

NOODLES IN SPICY COCONUT CURRY WITH SHRIMP

BEEF RENDANG

Beef Rendang

▲▲▲▲▲▲

5 lb (2½ kg) braising beef
3 tablespoons vegetable oil
2 large onions, sliced finely
8 cloves garlic, peeled
2 large onions, chopped roughly
1¼ inch (3 cm) piece fresh ginger, peeled
2 lemon grass stalks, trimmed and
halved lengthwise
2 x 14 fl oz (440 ml) cans thick coconut
milk (cream)
2 teaspoons ground turmeric
3 teaspoons chili flakes
1 tablespoon ground coriander
1½ teaspoons laos (galangal) powder
10 curry leaves
2 fresh red chilies, seeded and sliced
3 teaspoons tamarind concentrate
2 teaspoons brown sugar

Cut beef into 1¼ inch (3 cm) cubes and brown in 3 or 4 batches. Set aside. Brown the sliced onions in the same pan and set aside.

Place the roughly chopped onion, garlic, ginger and lemon grass in a food processor and grind to a paste. Transfer to the pan and sauté for 3-4 minutes, stirring to prevent sticking. Add 1 can of coconut milk and bring just to the boil. Reduce heat and simmer until the oil begins to separate, stirring from time to time to prevent catching on the pan.

Add meat and onions, spices, curry leaves and chilies to the pan with the remaining coconut milk and 2 cups water. Cover and cook for about 1½ hours until the meat is tender.

Stir in tamarind and sugar, add salt and pepper to taste and cook again gently until the meat is supremely tender and the sauce is reduced. Serve over rice.

RICE WITH GREEN PEAS AND ONION

Rice with Green Peas and Onion

▲▲▲▲▲▲

6 cups (30 oz / 900 g) long-grain white rice
1 tablespoon ground turmeric
1½ teaspoons chicken stock powder
¾ tablespoons toasted slivered almonds
3 cups (17 oz / 540 g) green peas
1 large onion, sliced finely
2 tablespoons ghee (clarified butter)

Rinse the rice, pour into a heavy saucepan and add turmeric and stock powder. Add water to cover by 1¼ inch (3 cm) and cover tightly. Bring briskly to the boil, then reduce heat to lowest temperature setting and allow the rice to cook undisturbed for 10 minutes. Stir once and cook a further 8 minutes, then stir again, cover and set aside.

Cook peas in very lightly salted water until tender, drain. Sauté the onion in three-quarters of the ghee until soft and lightly browned.

Butter a glass dish with the remaining ghee. Stir half the almonds into the rice. Spread one-third of the rice into the dish. Cover with peas. Spread one-third of the rice over the peas and cover with the onions. Spread the remaining rice over the onions and scatter the almonds onto it.

Cover with a piece of aluminum foil and warm in a moderately hot oven for 12 minutes before serving.

Guava Mousse with Fruit Salad

▲▲▲▲▲▲

2 cups (16 fl oz / 500 ml) guava juice
2 tablespoons gelatine
11 fl oz (600 ml) thick (heavy) cream
few drops rose pink food coloring
4 large bananas
1 lemon or large lime
1 fresh pineapple or 14 oz (450 g) canned pieces
2 red apples
2 large pears
3 oranges or 1 can mandarin segments
3-4 passionfruit
13 oz (400 g) can peaches or sliced mango

**Coconut Milk and Sugar Syrup
(optional topping):**
14 fl oz (440 ml) can thick coconut
milk (cream)
½ teaspoon salt
3 tablespoons crumbled palm or demerara sugar

Pour the guava juice into a bowl. Dissolve the gelatine in ½ cup boiling water and pour over the juice. Stir, then refrigerate until just at setting point.

Whip the cream to soft peaks. Whip the guava jelly until frothy and fold in the cream. Spoon into dessert glasses or small glass dishes and return to the refrigerator to set.

Peel and dice the banana and sprinkle on lemon or lime juice. Peel and dice the remaining fruit. Mix together and chill well.

The dessert can be served just with the fruit salad, or with coconut milk and brown sugar syrup to give it a truly Asian taste. Boil the coconut milk with salt until reduced and thickened, cool. Separately boil the sugar with 3 tablespoons water for 3 minutes, cool. To serve, top each with a portion of fruit salad, pour on a little of the coconut milk and sugar syrup.

GUAVA MOUSSE WITH FRUIT SALAD

ANYONE FOR COCKTAILS ?

Serves 20

Quail Egg Toasts

Sweetcorn Fritters

Crisp Crabmeat Balls

Thai-style Fishcakes

Yakitori Chicken

Vietnamese Chicken and Crabmeat Rolls

Curry Puffs

Empanadillas

Nori Maki Sushi

Satay Eggs

Cold Shrimp with Horseradish Mayonnaise

Fruit Kebabs with Yogurt Dip

Miniature Lamb Kebabs with Yogurt Dip

Crispy Chicken Fillets

Tiny nibbles from Asia add interest to cocktail party food. Each of these recipes makes at least 20 portions, so you can mix, match and multiply to cater for as many as you please. Allow four to eight hors d'oeuvre per guest.

Plan your menu, selecting hot and cold dishes to suit the occasion. Avoid choosing too many that require on-the-spot attention unless you have a skilled team in the kitchen.

131

A champagne that is not too dry is ideal with these Oriental tastes, or you might choose a dry, crisp champagne-style white wine and add a dash of Midori or peach liqueur. There are also many cocktails evocative of Asia which should make your party memorable – Pink Gin, Singapore Sling, Suntory Lady (whiskey and Midori) and Sake Cocktail (sake, Midori and vodka), or iced sake with a twist of lemon.

Quail Egg Toasts

▲▲▲▲▲▲

6 slices sandwich bread
2 dozen quail eggs
3 oz (90 g) fatty pork, diced
3 oz (250 g) shrimp meat
1 teaspoon grated fresh ginger
4 water chestnuts, chopped very finely
½ scallion (spring onion), chopped very finely
½ teaspoon salt
¼ teaspoon white pepper
1-2 tablespoons very finely minced (ground) ham
oil for deep-frying
chopped parsley (optional)

Stack bread slices, remove crusts and cut each slice into four squares.

Peel the quail eggs and set aside. Place pork, shrimp, grated ginger, water chestnuts and scallion in a food processor and process to a smooth paste, adding salt and pepper.

Place an egg on the middle of each piece of bread and cover it with filling. Bring the filling right to the edges of the bread to completely encase the egg. Press a little chopped ham onto each.

Heat oil and deep-fry the toasts, egg-side downward, until golden. Turn and cook the toast side briefly. Retrieve with a slotted spoon and drain on absorbent paper. Sprinkle with chopped parsley and serve hot with a sweet chili or sweet and sour dip.

Sweetcorn Fritters

▲▲▲▲▲▲

14 oz (440 g) can sweetcorn kernels, drained
(reserve liquid)
1 red salad (Spanish) onion, chopped very finely
2 cloves garlic, chopped very finely
1¼ teaspoons salt
½ teaspoon cracked black pepper
1-2 teaspoons chili sauce
2 large eggs, lightly beaten
⅔ cup self-raising flour
½ teaspoon baking powder
8 fresh spinach leaves, very finely chopped
oil for deep-frying

In a bowl, combine the ingredients except the oil and mix thoroughly, adding enough of the reserved liquid to make a thick batter. Set aside for 30 minutes.

Heat oil in a wok or pan suited to deep-frying. Fry dessertspoons of the batter until golden brown and floating on the surface, retrieve and drain on absorbent paper.

Pierce each with a toothpick (small wooden pick) and arrange on a platter around dishes of sweet and hot chili sauce.

SWEETCORN FRITTERS AND CRISP CRABMEAT BALLS

Crisp Crabmeat Balls

▲▲▲▲▲▲

¼ lb (120 g) fresh shrimp meat
2 cups fresh white breadcrumbs
½ lb (250 g) cooked crabmeat, flaked
2 tablespoons very finely chopped scallion
(spring onion)
½ teaspoon hot mustard powder
2 teaspoons lemon juice
½ teaspoon salt
1 teaspoon sugar
2 beaten eggs
oil for deep-frying

Bat the shrimp meat with the side of a cleaver blade to pulverize it. Place in a mixing bowl with two-thirds of the breadcrumbs, the crabmeat, scallion and seasonings. Mix well, work in the eggs and knead the mixture through the fingers until thoroughly blended.

Form into walnut-sized balls. Spread the remaining breadcrumbs on a plate and roll the balls over it to coat evenly. Chill for 30 minutes.

Heat oil in a large pan or wok. Deep-fry the crabmeat balls until crisp and golden and floating to the surface. Drain well and serve hot. Tomato ketchup spiked with Worcestershire and chili sauces makes an excellent accompaniment.

Thai-style Fishcakes

▲▲▲▲▲▲

7 oz (200 g) boneless and skinless white fish
1 teaspoon chopped fresh ginger
1 scallion (spring onion), trimmed
1 clove garlic, peeled
2½ teaspoons chopped lemon grass
½ fresh green chili, seeded
3 teaspoons Thai fish sauce
salt and white pepper
½ teaspoon sugar
1 small egg
2 teaspoons lemon juice
2 teaspoons cornstarch (cornflour)
¼ cup green beans or long (snake) beans, sliced paper-thin
oil for shallow-frying

Place the fish, ginger, scallion, garlic, lemon grass and chili in a food processor and process to a smooth paste. Add fish sauce, seasonings, sugar, egg, lemon juice and cornstarch and process again until thoroughly blended. Stir in the beans.

Heat oil in a wide, flat pan. Fry teaspoons of the mixture until golden underneath. Turn and fry the other side until the cakes are golden and feel firm. Remove and drain. Pierce each with a cocktail stick and serve hot with Thai sweet chili sauce or a hot spicy sauce.

YAKITORI CHICKEN

Yakitori Chicken

▲▲▲▲▲▲

1 lb (500 g) boneless, skinless chicken breast
120 g / 4 oz chicken livers
12 small pickling onions, peeled
3 tablespoons light soy sauce
2 tablespoons sake
1 tablespoon mirin (Japanese sherry) or dry sherry
1½ tablespoons sugar
Japanese shichimi pepper seasoning or cracked black pepper
thin bamboo skewers soaked in oil
vegetable oil

Cut the chicken and livers into bite-sized pieces. Blanch the onions in boiling water for 2 minutes, then drain well. Thread the ingredients alternately onto the skewers.

In a small saucepan, boil the soy sauce, sake, sherry and sugar for 2-3 minutes and set aside.

Brush the skewered ingredients lightly with oil and grill until the surface is seared. Brush with the glaze and return to the grill. Continue brushing and glazing until the meat is cooked.

Arrange on a platter and sprinkle on the pepper.

THAI-STYLE FISHCAKES

Vietnamese Chicken and Crabmeat Rolls

▲▲▲▲▲▲

12 sheets banh trang (edible rice paper)
1 tablespoon light corn syrup or a syrup of brown
sugar boiled with water
oil for deep-frying
180 g / 6 oz very finely minced chicken breast
3 oz (90 g) cooked crabmeat, flaked
2 scallions (spring onions), chopped very finely
30 g / 1 oz rice vermicelli, soaked
1 small carrot, finely grated
1 medium egg, beaten
salt and cracked black pepper
2 teaspoons cornstarch (cornflour)

Sauce Dip:
Combine the following:
1 tablespoon lime juice
3 tablespoons Vietnamese fish sauce
2 tablespoons water
sugar to taste
1 teaspoon very finely chopped fresh red chili
2-3 teaspoons crushed roasted peanuts

Dip the rice paper into cold water to soften, then spread on a cloth and cover with a damp cloth while the filling is prepared. Heat oil in large pan or wok.

In a mixing bowl combine the remaining ingredients for the filling, kneading with the fingers to mix thoroughly.

Cut rice papers in half. Brush one side with the corn syrup thinned with water, or use prepared caramel syrup. Turn halved rice papers over and place a portion of the filling in the middle. Fold in half over the filling to give a triangle with one curved side. Fold the two points over the filling, then beginning at the curved edge, roll down towards the point. Brush on a little extra syrup to stick it down. Keep the rolls covered while preparing the remainder.

Deep-fry in the hot oil until the surface is crisp and golden brown, drain well and serve with the sauce in a small dish for dipping.

VIETNAMESE CHICKEN AND CRABMEAT ROLLS

CURRY PUFFS

Curry Puffs

▲▲▲▲▲▲

1 medium onion, chopped very finely
½ lb (250 g) minced (ground) beef or lamb
½ inch (1.5 cm) piece fresh ginger, chopped very
finely
2 tablespoons vegetable oil or ghee
1 cup (6 oz / 180 g) diced cooked potato
½ cup (1½ oz / 45 g) cooked green peas
½ cup (2 oz / 60 g) cooked diced carrots
1 tablespoon mild curry powder or 2 teaspoons
garam masala
1 tablespoon finely chopped fresh
coriander or mint
1½ teaspoons salt
½ teaspoon black pepper
4-5 tablespoons water
1 pack frozen puff pastry, thawed
1 beaten egg
cayenne or paprika

Sauté the onion until lightly browned, add the meat and ginger and sauté until the meat changes appearance. Add the vegetables and curry powder or garam masala and cook for 1 minute, stirring continually. Add herbs, seasonings and water and simmer uncovered, until the liquid has completely evaporated.

Preheat an oven to 360°F (180°C). Sprinkle flour lightly over a board. Roll the pastry thinly and cut into 3 inch (8 cm) rounds. Place a portion of filling in the middle of each. Moisten the edges with beaten egg, fold over and press edges together. Use the points of a fork to decorate and seal the edges.

Brush the top surface of each curry puff lightly with beaten egg and sprinkle on cayenne or paprika. Place on a baking sheet or cookie tray and bake for about 18 minutes until golden brown. Allow to cool for 2 minutes on the tray, then serve.

Empanadillas

▲▲▲▲▲▲

1 package frozen puff pastry
¼ lb (120 g) smoked ham, chopped finely
1 medium onion, chopped finely
1 celery stalk, chopped finely
1 clove garlic, chopped finely
1 tablespoon vegetable oil
1 cup (4 oz / 120 g) cooked green peas
2 tablespoons finely chopped red pepper
(capsicum)
2 tablespoons sweet chili sauce
1 teaspoon tomato paste
⅓ teaspoon salt
¼ teaspoon black pepper
oil for deep-frying (optional)
egg for glazing pastry (optional)

Pastry:
2 ¾ cups (13 oz / 420 g) all-purpose (plain) flour
¾ teaspoon salt
3 tablespoons vegetable oil
iced water

Thaw frozen pastry or prepare the pastry recipe by sifting flour and salt into a mixing bowl. Make a well in the middle and add oil and enough water to make a slightly firm dough. Knead for 5 minutes, cover and let sit for 10 minutes.

Sauté ham, onion, celery and garlic in the oil for 3-4 minutes, add peas and red pepper and sauté briefly. Add the chili sauce, tomato paste and seasonings and mix well. Allow to cool.

Roll out the pastry on a floured board until very thin. Cut into 3 inch (8 cm) rounds. Place a portion of the filling in the middle of each and moisten the edges. Fold into a half moon and pinch the edges together, or use a fork to decorate and seal.

Arrange on a greased and floured baking tray, glaze with beaten egg and bake in a preheated oven at 360°F (180°C) for 18-20 minutes – or heat oil and deep-fry the pastries until they are golden brown and crisp. Drain well before serving. (Makes approximately 40.)

NORI MAKI SUSHI

Nori Maki Sushi

▲▲▲▲▲▲

Enhanced rice for sushi must be made within a few hours of serving, as the vinegar will make it begin to ferment after a short time. Do not refrigerate sushi rice or its texture will be spoiled. Completed nori maki rolls can be made in advance and refrigerated in a sealed container.

3 cups washed and thoroughly drained
short-grain white rice
3 ¾ cups (30 fl oz / 875 ml) water
3 inch (8 cm) piece kombu (dried kelp), rinsed
⅓ cup (3 fl oz / 85 ml) rice vinegar *
½ cup fine white sugar
3 teaspoons salt
1 medium cucumber
4 dried black mushrooms, soaked

1 medium carrot
2 eggs
½ teaspoon sake
¼ teaspoon salt
2 teaspoons vegetable oil
1 pack dried nori seaweed
pickled ginger shreds
* You may be able to purchase powdered seasoning for sushi where Japanese ingredients are sold.

Pour rice and water into a saucepan with a heavy base and tight-fitting lid. Add the kelp which has been scored on the surface with a sharp knife to release its seasoning. Cover and bring rapidly to the boil, then reduce heat and cook on lowest temperature setting for 18 minutes. Do not remove the lid until after cooking. Turn off the heat, place a folded towel over the saucepan and allow the rice to stand a further 12 minutes.

Combine the rice vinegar, sugar and salt in a small bowl and stir to dissolve the sugar. Use a wide, flat spoon to slowly turn the rice, adding the vinegar mixture in a very slow stream. Keep turning until all of the seasoning has been added, then transfer the rice to a large bowl and continue to stir it until it is cool. Cover and set aside.

Cut the cucumber lengthwise into narrow strips, discarding the fleshy central core and seeds, then cut into long shreds. Bring the mushrooms to boil in the liquid in which they were soaked, simmer for 6-7 minutes, then drain and remove stems. Shred the caps finely and set aside.

Cut the carrot into pieces similar to those of the cucumber. It can be used fresh or 'pickled' by sprinkling generously with salt and leaving for 10 minutes, then rinsing and marinating in a mixture of vinegar and sugar for another 10-20 minutes. Drain before use.

Beat the eggs well, adding 1 tablespoon of water and the sake and sugar. Pour oil into a small sauté pan and add the egg. Cook on low heat until the egg is lightly golden, then turn and cook the other side just long enough to firm the omelette. Remove from heat and leave to cool, then cut into long shreds.

To assemble the nori maki, hold sheets of nori seaweed over a flame until they crisp and turn darker, which will take just a few seconds. Place on a small bamboo mat for making sushi, or on a kitchen cloth. Cover with an even layer of rice, about ⅓ inch (1 cm) thick, and press it on firmly with moistened fingers.

Arrange the fillings along the middle of the rice and use the mat or cloth to roll the rice and seaweed around the filling. When the rolls are complete, squeeze them gently into shape and wrap firmly in a cloth, set aside for 10 minutes. Nori maki can be wrapped in clingwrap or placed in a sealed container and refrigerated for up to 8 hours.

To serve, cut the rolls into 1 inch (3 cm) pieces and arrange on a platter with small dishes of tamari soy sauce enhanced with finely grated ginger.

Satay Eggs

▲▲▲▲▲▲

10 small eggs, hard-boiled
1-1⅓ tablespoons bottled satay sauce
3 large lettuce leaves
small coriander or parsley sprigs
1 medium cucumber

Peel the eggs, cut in halves lengthwise and remove a sliver from the base of each so they will stand firmly. Use a teaspoon to carefully remove the yolks to a small mixing bowl. Mash with the satay sauce, then fill into a piping bag fitted with a large star nozzle.

Pipe stuffing into the egg whites and arrange them on a serving platter which has been lined with finely shredded lettuce. Place a sprig of herbs on each egg.

Score the skin of the cucumber lengthwise with a fork and cut into thin slices. Overlap them around the edge of the platter, then chill briefly before serving.

SATAY EGGS

COLD SHRIMP WITH HORSERADISH MAYONNAISE AND FRUIT KEBABS WITH YOGURT DIP

Cold Shrimp with Horseradish Mayonnaise

▲▲▲▲▲▲

24 medium-sized fresh shrimp, in their shells
¾ cup mayonnaise
1¼ teaspoons wasabi (Japanese horseradish)
2 teaspoons lemon juice
thin bamboo skewers

Place the shrimp in a steamer and steam over simmering water for about 6 minutes, drain and leave to cool.

Shell the shrimp, removing their heads but leaving the tails intact. Pass a skewer into the middle back of each shrimp, hook it upward to secure the dark vein and ease out to discard.

Pass a skewer along the length of each shrimp to straighten it. Arrange them on a platter.

Whisk mayonnaise, wasabi and lemon juice together and spoon into a dip dish, place in the middle of the platter and serve.

Fruit Kebabs with Yogurt Dip

▲▲▲▲▲▲

2 large bananas, peeled
2 carambola (star fruit), optional
2 nashi (Japanese pears)
2 mangoes, peeled
1 small pineapple
1 lemon
1 cup (8 fl oz / 250 ml) natural yogurt
3 tablespoons thick (heavy) cream
⅓ teaspoon ground ginger
½ teaspoon ground cinnamon
½ teaspoon black pepper
2 teaspoons honey

Slice bananas and carambola, and cut the remaining fruit, except lemon, into cubes. Thread onto thin bamboo skewers and squeeze on lemon juice to prevent the fruit browning.

In a bowl, beat the yogurt and cream, incorporating the spices and honey. Spoon into a dish suitable for dipping.

Miniature Lamb Kebabs with Yogurt Dip

▲▲▲▲▲▲

1½ lb (650 g) lean, boneless lamb
1½ teaspoons salt
½ teaspoon black pepper
2 tablespoons lemon juice
3 tablespoons natural yogurt
2 teaspoons garam masala spice mix
vegetable oil or ghee (clarified butter)
thin bamboo skewers, soaked in water

Cut the lamb into ½ inch (1.5 cm) cubes. Place in a dish and add the remaining ingredients except oil or ghee. Mix well and leave for 3-4 hours.

Heat a charcoal broiler (grill) until the coals glow red. Thread the lamb onto the skewers, three or four pieces to each skewer. Broil (grill), turning frequently and brushing with oil or ghee to prevent drying. The surface of the kebabs should be well crisped, but ensure they do not overcook.

Serve on a platter with a bowl of yogurt sauce in the middle, for dipping.

Yogurt Sauce:
1 cup (8 fl oz / 250 ml) natural yogurt
1 tablespoon thick (heavy) cream
½ small onion, chopped very finely

1 tablespoon chopped fresh mint leaves
1 teaspoon cumin seeds
½ teaspoon salt
¾ teaspoon sugar

Beat the ingredients together and chill until ready to serve.

CRISPY CHICKEN FILLETS

Crispy Chicken Fillets

▲▲▲▲▲▲

24 pieces chicken fillet (breast)
1 tablespoon mild curry powder
2 teaspoons chili sauce
salt and white pepper
1 cup (3½ oz / 100 g) self-raising flour
2 eggs, beaten
2 cups (5 oz / 150 g) shredded coconut
oil for deep-frying

Arrange the chicken fillets side-by-side on a flat dish. Combine the curry powder, chili sauce and seasonings. Spread evenly over the chicken and set dish aside for 20 minutes.

Make a batter of the flour, eggs and iced water. Coat the chicken and then dip into the coconut. Refrigerate for 1 hour.

Heat oil for deep-frying and fry the chicken pieces, about six at a time, until golden and crisp. Drain on absorbent paper and serve hot.

MINIATURE LAMB KEBABS WITH YOGURT DIP

GLOSSARY

Azuki Beans: These small, dull-red beans are often used in sweet Japanese dishes. Available dried and cooked in cans.

Banh Trang Rice Papers: These semi-transparent round sheets, resembling plastic and brittle when dry, are used as edible wrappers. In cold water they soften and become opaque, with a tendency to stick together.

Beancurd: A soft cake of boiled and pureed soy beans and setting agent which is highly nutritious and protein-rich. It is best when soft in texture and delicate in taste. Fresh beancurd lasts only a few days. Keep refrigerated.

Bean Pastes: Assorted Chinese seasoning pastes, made from fermented and processed soy beans, are available at Chinese grocers. Sweet bean paste (Hoisin Sauce) resembles a sweet barbecue sauce. Yellow bean paste is extremely salty and chili bean paste is both hot and salty. Store refrigerated.

Candlenut (Kemiri): A fibrous, dry-textured nut of buff color, resembling a macadamia. Used to season and thicken Indonesian curries.

Cardamom Pods: Light green seed pods containing brown-black, highly aromatic seeds that are used in a variety of Indian dishes. Whole pods are preferable to ground cardamom. Bruise them to release their taste.

Chickpea Flour (Besan): A fine yellow flour of ground chickpeas (garbanzos), which is used in Indian vegetarian cooking. Corn meal could be substituted.

Chilies, Chili Products: Fresh chilies, chili powder, sauce, flakes and pastes all vary in heat. Use sparingly, adding more during cooking if needed. Fresh chilies are milder once the seeds are removed. Wear plastic gloves to prepare.

Chinese Cabbage (Nappa): A large, tightly packed and delicate tasting cabbage that can be braised or simmered. The leaves are thick and creamy white at the base and pale green with crinkled edges at the top.

Coconut Milk: Available dried, compressed, fresh and canned. These recipes used the canned variety, specifying 'thin' for a standard coconut milk and 'thick' or 'cream' when a concentrated coconut milk is required. Freeze unused coconut milk as it quickly turns rancid.

Coriander: A spice and herb. The small, ocher seeds have a fresh, lemony taste which is used in curries. For full taste, toast and grind whole seeds in preference to the preground spice. The leaves (fresh) have a distinctive taste that is not suited to all palates. They are also known as Chinese parsley and cilantro.

Cumin: A slightly pungent spice used in curries. Toast and grind whole seeds for the best taste.

Dashi: This stock, the base of most Japanese sauces and soups, is made by infusing shaved, fried bonito fish and kombu seaweed. It is available in sachet packs of instantly dissolving granules.

Fish Sauce: Known in Vietnam as *nuoc mam* and in Thailand as *nam pla*, this is a salty, clear, amber sauce of processed brine-fermented fish.

Fungus: Dried black fungus (wood ears or tree ears) and white fungus (silver or snow fungus) should be soaked before use, and will expand to at least four times their dried size.

Galangal: A type of ginger, also called laos powder, which is used fresh or ground, particularly in Thai curries.

Garam Masala Spice Mix: Black peppercorns, coriander, cumin, cinnamon, cloves and cardamoms make up this aromatic, sweet spice mixture, used to season Indian curries.

Ghee (Clarified Butter): Pure yellow butterfat made by boiling and separating the water and impurities from butter. Substitute butter, margarine, or vegetable oil if preferred.

Kaffir Lime Leaves: Usually sold dried, should be soaked before use. Fresh citrus leaves can be substituted.

Lemon Grass: These slender shoots of citronella have a distinctive lemon taste and aroma. Use only the lower white or tightly packed pale green portion, halving lengthwise or chopping to release its taste. Its leaves make a calming, refreshing tea. Chopped, dried lemon grass is a reasonable substitute.

Mirin: A sweet, viscous, Japanese liquor that resembles sherry. Before use, boil it to concentrate the taste. Substitute a good, sweet sherry.

Oyster Sauce: A dark brown, thick strong and salty sauce processed from sun-dried oysters. It is used sparingly to season Chinese cooking, or more often, offered as a condiment on vegetable dishes.

Palm Sugar: Dark brown, crumbly sugar which gives a rich taste to many Asian dishes. Substitute a very dark brown sugar.

Pandan Leaf: The long deep-green leaves of the pandanus plant add color and a unique taste to certain dishes: check the freezer of your Chinese greengrocer. If unavailable, omit this ingredient as dried pandan leaves are not a satisfactory substitute.

Sambal Ulek: A salty, extremely hot Indonesian chili paste.

Seaweed: Giant tangle kelp (kombu) seasons stocks and sauces. Curly seaweed (wakame) can be a vegetable in salads or soups. Square sheets of nori, a compressed and dried sea plant, make edible wrappers for sushi or can be shredded as a garnish. Store carefully away from moisture.

Sesame Oil: Pressed from sesame seeds, this deep brown oil has a distinctive nutty taste and aroma and is used more as a condiment and seasoning than as a frying oil.

Shrimp Paste: Many types of shrimp paste are used in Asian cooking for their pungent taste and saltiness. Pink-grey Chinese shrimp sauce is mild and aromatic and used mostly with vegetables. Compressed shrimp paste (blachan) used in Malaysian recipes is a very pungent, dark brown, dryish cake which should be used sparingly and stored in a well-sealed jar.

Sichuan Brown Peppercorns: Vital to the characteristic taste of many Sichuan dishes, these aromatic red-brown dried berries are strong and peppery.

Soy Sauce: An extensively used, salty seasoning sauce and condiment. Tamari soy (Japanese) is salt-free, while the Indonesian sweet soy sauce contains palm sugar syrup.

Tamarind: A tart ingredient which heightens taste. It is sold in blocks containing seeds as well as yellow-brown fruit pulp. Remove seeds and dissolve pulp in water before using. Bottled pure tamarind or concentrated tamarind can be added directly to a dish.

Vermicelli: Semi-transparent vermicelli made from mung bean flour cooks to a slightly crunchy texture and appears in braised dishes and soups. Snowy white rice vermicelli is soft and subtle in taste and is used extensively in Asian dishes.

Vinegar: Where recipes specify white vinegar, use common, distilled white vinegar. Chinese brown (black) is used for its rich taste in certain dishes and Chinese red vinegar is preferred as a condiment. Substitute rice vinegar, which is mild in taste, in any of these recipes.

Wasabi: A Japanese ingredient of green paste or powder with super-hot taste made from a variety of horseradish and served as a condiment. Sold in small jars, tins and tubes.